THE
TENTMAKING
PASTOR

THE
TENTMAKING
PASTOR

THE JOY OF
BIVOCATIONAL
MINISTRY

Dennis W. Bickers

Baker Books
A Division of Baker Book House Co
Grand Rapids, Michigan 49516

© 2000 by Dennis Bickers

Published by Baker Books
a division of Baker Book House Company
P.O. Box 6287, Grand Rapids, MI 49516-6287

Second printing, August 2000

Printed in the United States of America

Library of Congress Cataloging-in-Publication Data

Bickers, Dennis W., 1948–
    The tentmaking pastor : the joy of bivocational ministry / Dennis W. Bickers.
        p.   cm.
    Includes bibliographical references.
    ISBN 0-8010-9099-7 (pbk.)
    1. Baptists—Clergy—Secular employment. I. Title.
BV676.5.B53   2000
253'.2—dc21   99-059734

For current information about all releases from Baker Book House, visit our web site:
http://www.bakerbooks.com

CONTENTS

ACKNOWLEDGMENTS

I want to acknowledge several people who made it possible for me to write this book. My editor, Paul Engle, at Baker Books offered me much encouragement and help during the process of writing my first book. I certainly appreciate his patience and kindness.

The wonderful people of Hebron Baptist Church have shown even greater patience over the past eighteen years I have served as their pastor. No pastor has ever received more love and affirmation than I have from these people. I consider myself truly blessed by God to have been called to this place of service.

Words cannot express my love and appreciation for my family. Our daughter and son, Melissa and Tim, have been everything a father could want in his children. And now they have given us grandchildren!

For thirty-three years my wife, Faye, has been my best friend and the love of my life. She has encouraged me, prayed for me, supported me, and loved me unconditionally. No bivocational pastor can succeed without the support of his family, and mine has certainly given me that support.

I want to dedicate this book to Faye, Melissa, and Tim. Thank you for your love and for the freedom to fulfill God's call on my life to be a bivocational pastor. I love you guys.

PREFACE

I was sitting in a chair in the front of the church facing the search committee. The few questions they asked dealt with what I would do as their pastor. At the end of our meeting, they knew nothing of my theological beliefs, but that did not seem to be of primary importance to this committee. What was important was summed up by one of the last questions. An older woman, her voice revealing great emotion, asked, "Do you think there is any hope for this little church?"

Soon after this meeting the church called me as their next pastor, despite the fact that I had no educational preparation nor did I have any experience except for a five-month term as interim pastor at a neighboring church. I might not have accepted the call if I had known that when the previous pastor left, many in the church struggled with the question, Do we try one more pastor, or do we lock the doors and join other churches?

That was eighteen years ago, and I am still the pastor of that same church—Hebron Baptist Church in Madison, Indiana. This book will *not* tell you how we went from those difficult beginnings to a church with thousands of members; we average about fifty people on Sunday mornings. This book *will* tell you, however, how rewarding, meaningful, and challenging bivocational ministry is. It will describe how God can use a small church to touch its community and how he will bless the church in that process.

A bivocational minister is one who has a secular job as well as a paid ministry position in a church. Bivocational ministry is sometimes referred to as tentmaking ministry because our biblical example for bivocational ministry is the apostle Paul, who supported himself financially by making tents. In Acts 18:2–4 we read that Paul stayed with Aquila and Priscilla in Corinth because they were also tentmakers. The three of them worked together during the week, and Paul would then minister in the synagogue every Sabbath.

As a tentmaker, Paul had a marketable skill that was needed wherever God might lead him to minister. It appears that Paul continued to make tents as he traveled from city to city. In his letters to the Corinthians (1 Cor. 4:12; 2 Cor. 11:7–9) and the Thessalonians (1 Thess. 2:9; 2 Thess. 3:8), Paul reminds readers that he was not a financial burden to them as he ministered in their cities; with his own hands he provided for his physical needs.

While reading the above passages of Scripture, one can sense that Paul felt a measure of satisfaction in not being a financial burden to the people he ministered to and loved. I frequently encounter that same satisfaction when talking to modern-day tentmaking pastors. These pastors often comment about the things their churches are able to do because they do not have to spend a great deal of money on pastoral support. They are glad to be bivocational because their churches, often small in size, are financially able to offer ministries to their communities.

My heart goes out to small churches. Most of them are filled with godly people who want to grow in Christ and want to be used by him to make a difference in the lives of others. Limited resources and a lack of leadership sometimes limit what they are able to do. The frustration level in such churches is often high. Revolving-door pastoral leadership compounds the problems. A bivocational pastor, in addition to helping the financial situation of a small church, as mentioned above, can also provide the stability such a church needs to reach its potential simply because such a pastor will often stay at the church for a longer period of time than will a fully funded pastor. This allows a level of trust to be developed between the church members and the pastor that will lead to more effective ministry.

This more effective ministry is important for at least two reasons. First, every church is needed to fulfill the Great Commission that Christians were given by our Lord. Only China and India have more unsaved people than does the United States.[1] The church must find ways to reach the multitudes who do not have Jesus Christ in their lives. Michael Green reminds us that "whenever Christianity has been at its most healthy, evangelism has stemmed from the local church and has had a noticeable impact on the surrounding area. I do not believe that the re-Christianization of the West can take place without the renewal of local churches in this whole area of evangelism."[2]

The second reason is that every believer in Jesus Christ deserves quality ministry and instruction. People should not be penalized in their personal spiritual development because they attend a small church. Biblical teaching and opportunities for ministry should exist in every church regardless of size.

Bivocational ministry provides unique challenges for the church and the minister. Those challenges are discussed in this book. For the past eighteen years, our church and I have experienced most of them and found ways to overcome them. This book is written out of our experiences and is meant to be an encouragement to those who serve as bivocational pastors and to those who are members of bivocational churches.

Although I use masculine pronouns throughout the book when referring to pastors, the ideas shared in this book apply to female pastors as well. Since well over 90 percent of pastors are male, however, I chose to use masculine pronouns to facilitate easier reading. These pronouns are not meant to make a theological statement about female pastors or to demean their ministries.

I recently took early retirement after working thirty years in a local factory. Besides serving as a pastor for sixteen of those years, I also had responsibilities as a husband, a father, and a student. During my pastorate at Hebron Baptist Church, I graduated from Boyce Bible School and earned a bachelor's degree from an area university. I know how difficult it is to do bivocational ministry and have time for your family and yourself. Incidentally, my early retirement still did not allow me to devote all my time to the church. For the past two years I have also managed a small business my family owns.

There are few resources for the bivocational pastor. Books about small church ministry are helpful, but they seldom mention bivocational ministry. When I first began my ministry, the only book that addressed bivocational ministry was John Elliott's *Our Pastor Has an Outside Job* (Judson Press, 1980). The book primarily reviewed a study that had been done about bivocational ministry and offered some suggestions about how such a ministry could be established in a local church. The first book I found that offered some practical helps for the bivocational minister was Luther Dorr's *The Bivocational Pastor* (Broadman Press, 1988). The notes at the end of the book contain many resources that I have found helpful in my ministry.

It is my prayer that this book will be somewhat different from others I have read. I write from the perspective of one who has served in bivocational ministry for a number of years and who believes that God is using this type of ministry to do some wonderful things in his church. I want to encourage those of you who are now serving as bivocational pastors. I also want to inspire those who are considering bivocational ministry to carefully consider such a call. It is also my hope that church leaders of small churches will read this book before calling their next pastor. Finally, along with what I hope will be some practical advice, I want to share with you the *joy* of bivocational ministry.

ONE

BIVOCATIONAL MINISTRY IS REAL MINISTRY

I once heard a story about a little boy who was walking down a beach early one morning. The beach was covered with starfish the tide had brought in during the night. The boy was throwing the starfish back into the ocean when an older man walked up to the lad. "What are you doing?" he asked the boy.

"Throwing these starfish back into the ocean before they die," was the reply.

The man looked at the hundreds of starfish lying on the beach and then looked back at the young boy and laughed. "Do you really think what you are doing will make any difference?"

The little boy answered, "It makes a difference to this one," as he threw another starfish into the water.

Bivocational pastors sometimes wonder if their ministry really makes a difference. Thoughts such as the following are not uncommon:

> "If I were really called by God to pastor, he would call me to another (usually larger) church."
>
> "If I were a real pastor, we would have seen growth in this church by now."
>
> "I must not be doing something right. People's lives are just not being affected by anything I say or do."

Do any of these sound familiar? At one time or another I have said all these statements and many others like them. Most bivocational ministers have struggled with these issues.

Because people tend to measure success and worth with numbers, many believe that bivocational ministry is not real ministry. Most bivocational pastors serve in small churches. A dozen baptisms in a year would be cause to celebrate; most years we are thankful to baptize two or three. Visitors may come, but few return the following week. They are looking for a church with a choir, a larger youth group, or a special program. Finances are usually tight. If success is determined by large numbers, a bivocational ministry will seldom be considered successful.

THE PROBLEM OF SHORT PASTORATES

In our geographical area, there are a large number of small churches. Many of them are served by seminary students who seldom stay after graduation. The church I pastor, Hebron Baptist Church, had been served by student pastors for many years with the average pastorate lasting approximately eighteen months. The church had adopted the belief, common to many similar churches, that its value lay in being a training ground for student pastors. Even worse, many believed that they were not good enough to keep a pastor. A long-time member of Hebron commented that I would probably soon be leaving for a better church, and I had been pastor there for less than a year! I immediately knew this mind-set would have to change before the church could begin to move forward. Perhaps still worse was the amount of pain that had built up in people's hearts over the years and had not been shared with their transient pastors.

In his research, George Barna has found that the smaller the church, the more likely it is that a pastor will leave after a short ministry. This is unfortunate because his studies also show that the most productive time in a pastor's ministry is often between the third and fifteenth year of service to a church. Churches who experience frequent short pastorates are less likely to trust their pastors and will be less likely to be outreach oriented.[1] This creates a deadly cycle for the church. A new pastor comes to serve the church. The church does not trust his leadership and does not implement his suggestions for new programming. He feels that his ministry is not productive and begins looking for another place to serve. When he leaves after a short period of time, the church feels justified in their lack of trust in his leadership. The church calls a new pastor, and the cycle begins again. This cycle will not be broken until a pastor comes and stays until the necessary level of trust is developed. The church can then begin to move forward.

Short pastorates also contribute to the problem of biblical illiteracy that exists in many of our small churches today. We are encouraged in Acts 20:27 to preach "the whole counsel of God," and that cannot happen when a church has a new pastor every year or so.

Within a few weeks of being called as pastor of Hebron, I preached a sermon about the need for people to be ready for the rapture of the church. An individual who had been a member of our church for many years later told me she had never heard of the rapture. This individual was faithful in attending services every Sunday, but she had never heard a sermon about the rapture.

Student pastors often limit their preaching to the more familiar biblical texts. Certainly there is nothing wrong with preaching from such texts, unless, of course, these same messages are repeated every two years due to frequent pastoral changes. A pastor who is not in school but leaves a church after a short pastorate may do so because his sermon barrel has run dry. For some reason, some ministers can find only about three years' worth of sermons in the Bible. When those are used up, they need to move on to another church. Unfortunately, the ones who suffer are the members of those churches, who are deprived of solid, biblical teaching that will enable them to become disciples of the Lord Jesus Christ.

A longer pastorate can address the problem of biblical illiteracy if the pastor is willing to do the hard work of study in his sermon preparation. Many ministers find it helpful to preach a series of sermons. One series could be topical in nature, such as a series of sermons that deal with family issues. Every year I preach a series of such messages between Mother's Day and Father's Day.

Some ministers preach a series of expository messages that deal with specific characters in the Bible or that cover an entire book of the Bible. Donald Grey Barnhouse began his ministry as pastor of the Tenth Presbyterian Church in Philadelphia by preaching a sermon based on Romans 1:1. He never preached a sermon outside the Book of Romans for three and a half years.[2] One Sunday at the First Baptist Church of Dallas, Texas, the pastor, Dr. W. A. Criswell, preached on Genesis 1:1, intending to preach through every book of the Bible. Nearly eighteen years later he finished that series.[3] Each year I preach through a book or a major section of the Bible. This annual series has been well received by our congregation, who enjoy this type of in-depth Bible study.

Most members of small churches are not exposed to that type of biblical teaching because short pastorates do not lend themselves to long studies of individual books of the Bible. That's unfortunate because members of small churches are entitled to quality ministry and to sound biblical instruction. A ministry to a handful of people is just as important as a ministry to thousands, especially to the handful. The lost and hurting handful do not care if you minister to thousands; they are thankful you are there with them. While preparing my sermons, I know that I am not likely to change the world, but if I can minister to the handful God has given me, then I will be successful.

Another serious problem caused by short pastorates is the constant disruption a church feels when pastors come and go. One pastor has said, "Most psychologists would consider a family whose husband and father abandoned them every four or five years to be seriously dysfunctional."[4] Although there will usually be some pain involved whenever a pastor leaves his place of service, I doubt that many pastors consider the amount of residual pain a church carries due to frequent pastoral changes. This pain may well explain why small churches are resistant to change. Why should the church accept the new pastor's ideas when experience tells them he will soon be leaving for a new church? It is difficult for such a church to trust a new pastor when they feel they've been abandoned by previous pastors.

REASONS FOR SHORT PASTORATES
IN SMALL CHURCHES

Pastors leave small churches after a relatively short period of time for a variety of reasons. Often, the reason is financial. A recent graduate of a seminary may have a large school loan that must be repaid. A small church simply may not be able to pay an adequate salary to retire that debt and provide for the needs of the pastor's family.

According to a survey conducted by *Leadership* magazine, the 1996 median base salary for a solo pastor with a congregation of less than 50 people was $16,560. Pastors in churches with 101 to 150 people received salaries of $27,850.[5] These figures do not include housing allowances. When a housing allowance is included, the typical pastor receives a salary package of $32,049.[6] Most small churches are not able to provide that kind of salary for a pastor.

The Southern Baptist Convention has approximately seven thousand fully supported pastors serving in churches with less than sixty people in Sunday school attendance. Some of these pastors receive salaries that are near the minimum wage; some qualify for food stamps.[7] This creates unnecessary stress on the minister and his family. We should not be surprised, or critical, if God meets their needs by providing another place of service.

I mentioned earlier that some pastors leave after a short period of time because they have exhausted their supply of sermons. Unfortunately, the ministry is a great place for a lazy person to hide. There are no time clocks to punch, and few churches ask for an accounting of a minister's time. Rather than developing the discipline needed to study, it is easier for such a pastor to have a series of three-year pastorates that will take him to retirement. Whenever the sermon barrel is nearly empty, this pastor updates his profile and soon begins talking to other churches.

Some pastors do not stay at churches very long because the churches do not allow them to do so. These pastors are not fired because of some conflict in the church. Rather, some churches believe that a pastor should be at a church for a certain period of time and then move on to another church. I recently heard of one church who told their pastor that he should begin seeking another church because he was nearing his fifth year of service in that church. The church leadership believed five years was an appropriate length of service. Perhaps this is a way a church protects itself against the pain they have experienced when previous pastors have left. This may also be a way that the lay leadership in a church ensures that a pastor does not stay long enough to be a challenge to their leadership. Whatever the reason, it is an unfortunate occurrence for the pastor and the church.

The final reason I will mention is the most unfortunate of all. Some pastors feel that a small church is simply beneath their dignity. A few weeks after becoming the pastor of Hebron, I was shopping in a Christian bookstore. Another customer was asking an employee of the store if he had talked to any churches since his recent graduation from seminary. I will never forget his answer: "All the churches that have contacted me have been small churches out in the country. I am not going to waste my time on such churches. I would rather work here." Such an attitude has no place in the heart of a pastor.

There are no insignificant places of service. Each church, large or small, consists of God's children who need a shepherd. They need someone to lead them in worship and Bible study. They need someone to equip them for the work of ministry (Eph. 4:12). They need someone to represent God to them in times of grief and crisis. Members of small churches are just as entitled to quality ministry as are the members of large churches. How sad it is when a pastor believes otherwise.

BIVOCATIONAL PASTORS CAN STAY LONGER

Bivocational pastors can remain in their churches longer because they often do not face the financial pressures that a seminary graduate may face. Their church salary may be a small percentage of their total income. Some bivocational pastors actually give more back to the church in tithes and offerings than they receive in salary from the church.

Bivocational pastors may also stay longer because they are serving a church in or near their home community. On occasion a church will seek a bivocational pastor, hoping he will move to their community, find a job, and serve their church. All the bivocational pastors I know personally, however, are serving churches in or near their home communities. With the family established in the community and the pastor established in a second career, it is advantageous for the pastor to stay in one place for a longer period of time. This longer period of service benefits the church as well.

THE ADVANTAGE OF LONG PASTORATES

A long pastorate provides a continuity of ministry to a church that allows for stronger pastoral leadership. It provides more time

19

for a pastor to understand the needs of the people so sermons and ministry can speak to those needs. Only when a pastor is able to stay in a church for an extended period of time can he really begin to be identified with the church and with the community. This identification leads to perhaps the most important ingredient for an effective ministry: trust.[8]

I had been pastor at Hebron for about seven years when an individual asked to speak to me. During our conversation, I became aware that he was revealing personal and painful information about his life. This individual had known many pastors, but this was the first time he had been able to share with a pastor. I had stayed long enough for a level of trust to be established between us. Similar situations occurred with other people who longed to tell their stories to someone who would care and who would continue to love them.

Trust comes from spending time developing relationships with the members of a church. Doran McCarty reminds us that "the source of leadership in the small church for the pastor is in relationships rather than in some expertise."[9] Relationships do not automatically happen simply because an individual has been called as the pastor of a church. A pastor can enter into relationships only as he spends time in the lives of other people.

The apostle Paul modeled this in his ministry. For example, in 1 Thessalonians 2, he reminded the church of the type of relationship they shared while he was with them. He invested not only time but his very life into that church. An intimate relationship grew between the church and Paul based on love, integrity, and mutual respect. Paul loved the people as a nursing mother loves her child, and it is obvious they loved him in return.

As I mentioned in the preface, Paul ministered to the church as a bivocational minister. Not wanting to be a burden to the local church, he supported himself as a tentmaker (v. 9). He also did not want his critics to accuse him of preaching the gospel for money (vv. 5–6). Working night and day, Paul provided for his financial needs while developing intimate relationships with the

20

Thessalonican Christians that led to the growth of a great evangelistic church (1 Thess. 1:8).

The first time I visited one of the deacons of our church, he was in the barn working on a piece of farm equipment. Although he suggested we go to the house for our visit, I just turned a five-gallon bucket upside down, sat down on it, and told him we could visit while he finished his work. I had been raised on a farm, and it certainly was not the first time I had sat on a bucket in a barn. He laughed and said that I would probably do okay as pastor of their church. We had a wonderful visit that afternoon.

I had entered his world and was not uncomfortable in it. Trust had not yet occurred in such a short time, but steps had been taken that could, and did, lead to trust.

Many pastors of small churches become frustrated because they find their churches unwilling to change. The primary reason for such unwillingness is often that the pastor has not been there long enough for the church to trust him. The members of the church probably do not doubt his integrity, but they do doubt his commitment to their church. Experience tells them that he will soon be leaving them, and they will be left with the changes that were made.[10] People in small churches are willing to change only when they trust their pastor.

A friend of mine began a bivocational ministry in a church that asked him to concentrate on establishing a youth ministry in the church. He met with the young people of the church to determine how interested they were in having such a ministry. The young people were also asked what types of activities they would enjoy as a group. They were unanimous in wanting to go to a theme park in a nearby state. He promised to ask for approval at the next business meeting.

That meeting was his first as the pastor of the church. It went well until he mentioned the young people's interest in the trip. Several adults immediately let him know that their children would not be going on such a trip! He was shocked at the anger a seemingly simple request generated. The trip was refused, and the committee went on to other business.

A member of the church called the pastor later that evening and explained that the reaction to his request was due to an incident that had occurred several years earlier. Of course, he was unaware of the incident and the pain it had caused the church. After serving only a few weeks in the church, he did not have the church's trust to lead another group of young people on a trip.

Trust will eventually come but only after several years of ministry. At Hebron, we attempted small changes. When those were successful, the church was ready to try other changes. In time, even when changes were attempted that did not work out, the trust factor was not hurt. Hebron has been willing to try just about everything I have suggested. Sometimes they have worked as we hoped; other times they failed. But we have attempted them together.

Pastoral leadership depends on trust. Your ability to lead your church will be dependent on the level of trust the members of that church have for you. One of the key elements of that trust is the amount of time you are willing to invest in their lives.

A long pastorate enables a pastor to better understand the needs of the congregation so sermons can address those needs. Sermons need to be theologically sound and relevant to the needs of the listeners. A message detailing the lives of the Hittites may be historically and theologically accurate, but if it does not relate to the needs of the hearers, it is of little value. Only when a pastor knows his congregation can he prepare his sermons so they will be relevant to the needs of the congregation.[11]

There are some who criticize needs-based preaching,[12] but Rick Warren is correct when he notes that such preaching "is based on the theological fact that God chooses to reveal himself to man according to his needs."[13] Christ gave sight to the man born blind. He offered forgiveness to the woman caught in the act of adultery. In both the Old and New Testaments God met people at their point of need and led them to life-changing experiences. Members of small churches need to have their needs understood and addressed so God can work in their circumstances and lead them to the same life-changing experiences. Bivocational pastors who can remain in their churches for long tenures can help that happen.

The community may also benefit from the longer pastorate of a bivocational minister. Such a minister may be more likely to own his own home and be a permanent member of the community.[14] This can lead to a greater understanding of the community and its needs, which in turn can lead to more community involvement on the part of the pastor.

Our church is located in the same community in which my wife and I have lived most of our lives. Our children attended the same school from which we graduated, so it was natural for us to be involved in school functions. I spent several years coaching basketball and baseball teams in the summer. I am currently on the board of directors of our local youth shelter that provides a safe place to live and some important programs for troubled young people. Before taking early retirement from my job, I was a member of our plant's community relations committee. We met regularly to discuss various funding requests that came from many community and school groups and to determine which of these we would support financially. Serving on that committee enabled me to better understand the good work that many organizations were doing in our community. It also made me aware of the important community resources to which I can refer people who come to me in need of assistance.

As you can see, community involvement is a win-win situation for the community and for the bivocational pastor. The community can see that you are making investments in the well-being of the community. This adds credibility to your ministry and enables your ministry to have a much greater impact on the lives of more people. The pastor also wins because his involvement can lead to a better understanding of community resources available to those who come to him in need.

Bivocational ministry is real ministry because you are touching the lives of real people. You are entering their world, experiencing their joys and their pain, and believing with them that

23

God can make a difference. God may well permit you to remain at your place of ministry for a long period of time, allowing trust to develop between you and the church. This trust will enhance your leadership and allow for increased ministry by the church. As you become better acquainted with the members of your congregation, your sermons will speak to the issues they face in their lives. You may not reach thousands of people with your ministry, but as in the story of the little boy and the starfish told at the beginning of the chapter, your ministry will matter to those whose lives you do touch.

TWO A NEEDED MINISTRY

First Kings 19 contains a fascinating story about Elijah. He has just conquered the priests of Baal on Mount Carmel and demonstrated the power of God to the people of Israel. When word comes to him that Jezebel has vowed to take his life, he flees to the wilderness and prays that he might die. When God questions him, Elijah answers in verse 10, "I have been very zealous for the LORD God of hosts; for the children of Israel have forsaken Your covenant, torn down Your altars, and killed Your prophets with the sword. I alone am left; and they seek to take my life."

Sometimes ministry is a very lonely place. Bivocational pastors can feel even more alone because it often seems there is little support for what we do. Community ministerial meetings are often held during the day while we are at work. While other pastors are able to spend time together to support and encourage the work each is doing, we have to find that same support somewhere else after work. Denominational meetings are also frequently held during the day. I have been amused, and sometimes frustrated, at how often various denominations describe themselves as consisting of small churches, and yet many of their meetings are held when the bivocational pastors of those small churches cannot attend. It is easy for a bivocational pastor to feel that he is alone in his efforts to serve his church. The fact is, however, many of us have been called to bivocational ministry.

Approximately 12 percent of all Protestant pastors in the United States are bivocational.[1] The Southern Baptist Convention has approximately 13,000 bivocational pastors,[2] which means that roughly 30 percent of its churches are led by such pastors.[3] Some believe that out of all the Baptist churches in America, over 73 percent are led by bivocational ministers.[4] We should be encouraged as we realize that God has called many other people to bivocational ministry.

These numbers were much higher than I had anticipated, but I also believe we will see the percentage increase even more in the years to come. The Catholic Church has been forced to close some parishes because of a shortage of priests. Protestant churches may soon experience a similar shortage of trained clergy. Small churches will be unable to compete with large churches for the pastors who are available. Many of them may have to choose between calling a bivocational pastor or closing their doors.

Let's examine some of the reasons for this shortage of pastors and how bivocational pastors can help.

A SHORTAGE OF PASTORS

Church Planting

Various denominations are finding that new churches are the most effective means of reaching immigrants.[5] Many of these new churches are located in population areas where large numbers of immigrants gather when they first come to the United States. For example, a number of new churches have been planted in southern Florida to reach out to Haitians. These churches are often led by Haitian ministers and reflect the worship styles the Haitian people prefer. In California, similar new churches have been started to reach out to Japanese, Thai, and Vietnamese people. Many of these churches are growing because they eliminate cultural and language barriers that these people groups might encounter if they attended an established church.

New churches are also effective in reaching the large number of unchurched people who already live in the United States. Older, established churches are often more concerned with the care of their own members than they are in reaching out to the unchurched around them. Administrative duties, sermon preparation, committee meetings, and pastoral care of members often leave the pastor little time for outreach. Laypeople are also busy with the work they do in their churches. As a result, in many of our churches today, little outreach and evangelism are being done.

Some new churches are started for the express purpose of reaching out to unchurched people. Strategically located in areas with large numbers of such people, these churches offer programs and worship services designed to appeal to people who have not been reached by the established churches in the area. Most of the people who join these churches are new Christians or people who have not been involved in a church for a number of years.

In 1982, the American Baptist Churches/USA held a New Church Planting Convocation. After many more meetings and much prayer, in 1984, the denomination began a church planting program with the theme "500 More by '94." That goal was exceeded, and today a new American Baptist church is started in the United States every eight days.[6] American Baptists have a new vision now: one new church a week between now and the year 2001.[7]

Bivocational pastors can play an important role in the planting of new churches.[8] A person who already lives in the area in which a new church is being started will have an advantage over someone who must move in and learn about the community. Not only would he already know the community, he may also be one who is known and trusted by those within the community. Hebron certainly was not a new church start when I began my ministry there, but people I knew from the community have become active members of the church during my pastorate. I have also had the opportunity to share my faith with co-workers who have been able to watch me over the years and have decided to trust me with their questions or problems. It would take time for a new person to earn that trust.

A bivocational pastor can also help stretch the limited finances of a new church. Starting new churches costs money, and it can be a long time before a new church is self-supporting. No denomination has an unlimited amount of money available for new church development. Bivocational pastors need less money from the denomination or the church to support their families, which means more money is available to start other churches. Hiring a bivocational pastor may also help a marginal church stay alive long enough for it to survive on its own.

An Aging Ministry

Another factor that could lead to a greater need for bivocational ministers is the large number of older ministers and missionaries. In 1996, the first baby boomers turned fifty years of age, and two-thirds of current pastors are over forty.[9] In the next two decades, a large number of clergy will reach retirement age.

Although many seminaries are reporting increased enrollment, those students are not necessarily training for pastoral ministry. Many preparing for ministry today are planning to specialize in specific ministries such as counseling, hospital chaplaincy, and other fields not related to church ministry.[10]

A young man who served our church as a youth minister recently graduated from seminary and moved to another state with his wife, also a seminary graduate. He told me that rather than serving as a pastor, he wanted to work in a Christian camp or with a campus ministry. He and his wife are now working with deaf children in a care facility and leading occasional youth retreats. God has called them to a wonderful ministry, but their ministry demonstrates that not all who are now attending seminary are preparing for a pastoral ministry.

In the future, there are simply not going to be enough seminary trained pastors for all of our churches. Small churches, especially, are going to find it difficult to find—and keep—a fully funded, seminary trained pastor. If these churches want to enjoy the benefits of a long-term pastorate, they will need to consider calling a bivocational pastor.

An Aging Church

As churches age it is not uncommon for their memberships to decrease in number. Lyle Schaller reports that most churches that have passed their seventy-fifth birthday have seen their average attendance shrink.[11] Approximately 60 percent of all Protestant churches now average less than one hundred in attendance, and this percentage continues to grow as established churches continue to age. Few of these churches can afford a fully funded pastor. It is also doubtful that many of them will provide a fully funded pastor with a workload that will challenge him and make use of the gifts God has given him. For these reasons, older churches will find it increasingly more difficult to find and keep a fully funded pastor, and as a result, may experience a rapid turnover of ministers.

Why do older churches often experience declining attendance? Some of the reasons may include:

- resistance to change
- demographic changes in the community that are not reflected in the church
- weak pastoral and/or lay leadership
- focus on inward needs rather than those outside the church

29

A recurring theme in this book is that bivocational pastors can provide the stability a church needs because they can often remain at a church for a long period of time. While almost any church will benefit from long pastorates, for the declining church it is almost mandatory if the church wants to stop its decline and begin to grow. George Barna found that "one of the most basic requirements for a turnaround church was for the pastor to establish a bond of trust with the congregation."[12] That trust takes time to develop. Only when trust exists between the pastor and the membership of a church can the above problems be addressed and resolved.

Ministry Dropouts

H. B. London and Neil B. Wiseman have estimated that 40 percent of those who now serve in ministry positions in churches will not be doing so in ten years.[13] Apart from the reasons already mentioned above, some will leave the ministry due to burnout and stress.

Pastors feel stress from many sources:

- Economic stress results when pay is too low to adequately support one's family.
- Emotional stress can come when expectations are too high, either on the part of the church or the individual pastor.
- Family stress results when the demands of ministry rob the pastor and family of time spent together.
- Identity stress occurs when pastors believe their life's work is not making a difference.

Most of these stressors will be examined in greater detail in other places in this book, but let's take a look at how a bivocational pastor can avoid the identity stress that other pastors may face.

Men often find much of their identity and self-worth in their work. When two men meet for the first time, it is common for them to introduce themselves by telling what they do for a living. Many men also use work to prove something to themselves, their fathers, and other important people in their lives about their manhood and their ability to succeed in life.[14] Since a man's identity is so closely connected to his work, what happens to that identity when his work seems to lack meaning?

People entering the ministry usually do so for worthy reasons. They feel God has called them to a place where they can make a difference in the lives of other people. They often spend time in school preparing themselves for ministry. When they begin a pastorate they are filled with hopes and dreams of affecting the lives of those in their congregation.

While ministry certainly has its mountaintop experiences, it also has its valleys. A pastor may encounter apathy in the church. Because they "like our little church," members may oppose efforts to reach out to new people or develop new programs. Others may be openly critical of the pastor or his family. For the pastor who finds his self-worth in his work, this can be a critical time.

Like any other pastor, I have enjoyed the mountaintop experiences, and I have known the valley times of ministry as well. There have been Sunday afternoons when I knew my sermon that morning was inadequate. I have left meetings knowing I had failed to provide the leadership the church needed to move forward. I have been in conflict with members of the church that brought them and me much pain. Some have left the church because of me. More than once I have questioned whether the work was worth the pain I was feeling.

During these times, the advantage I had as a bivocational pastor was that my self-worth was not tied to my pastoral role. Monday morning I was back in the factory running my machine, or working on the assembly line, or responding to a customer in another country who had a problem with one of our products. Perhaps I had failed at a ministry task the day before, but that did not make me a failure as a person. My work that day at my other job proved that I was a competent person.

Incidentally, the reverse is also true. I have had bad days at my factory job when everything that could go wrong did. That evening, however, I may have had a wonderful experience during a hospital visit in which I was able to bring comfort to someone.

SOME CHURCHES RECOGNIZE THEIR NEED

Many churches now look specifically for bivocational pastors. Some of these churches are too small to compete financially with larger churches for the fully compensated pastors who are available. Other churches simply believe that a bivocational pastor may be the best person for their situation. These may be the types of churches about which Leith Anderson writes, "The church of the twenty-first century promises to place a premium on performance rather than on credentials. There is less concern over degrees, accreditation, ordination, and other credentials, but an increased asking of the practical question, 'Can he or she do the job?'"[15]

Lyle Schaller has noted that "the crucial criteria for the pulpit committee from the small church are not educational attainment, oratorical ability, academic records, scholarly achievements, or experience on denominational committees. This committee usually is seeking a pastor who genuinely loves people, is an extroverted personality, really enjoys being with people, and is a walking model of an adult Christian."[16]

Anderson lists some qualifications that he believes church leaders are going to need as we enter the twenty-first century. Bivocational pastors can possess all of these qualifications.

1. New leaders must be attuned to the culture.
2. New leaders must be flexible.
3. New leaders must be relational.
4. New leaders must be good communicators.
5. New leaders must be entrepreneurs.
6. New leaders must be risk takers.
7. New leaders must be godly.[17]

DENOMINATIONS MUST RECOGNIZE THE NEED

Although many churches recognize the need for bivocational pastors, some denominations have been slow to react to this need. One such denomination is the one in which I serve, the American Baptist Churches/USA. Several years ago, the American Baptist Churches adopted the master of divinity degree as the minimum educational standard required for ordination. Provision was made that allows a local church to ordain a minister who does not have that degree. The denomination, however, makes a notation in the denominational directory indicating that the educational standard has not been met by that particular individual. A local church ordination may not be recognized by another church if the minister leaves the region. If a candidate appears before a state ordination council without a master's degree, it is extremely unlikely the council will recommend the person for ordination.

Our local association's constitution provides for an associational ordination council that participates in a local church's ordination. When I requested ordination as the pastor of Hebron, the association called a council from the other churches to examine my beliefs. They made sure I understood that my lack of a master of divinity degree would permit me to receive only a local church ordination, and then we proceeded with the ordination. The service was very meaningful, and the association has always been supportive of my ministry at Hebron.

However, a year ago an attempt was made by the association to change the language in its constitution so it more closely matched national standards. A candidate would have to appear before the state ordination council for review of his qualifications and would be ordained only after a recommendation by that council. No provision was made for a local church ordination in the proposed changes.

I opposed the change because of my belief that bivocational pastors are going to be needed even more in the future than we are now. Because many of those pastors would not have a master of divinity degree, they would not have been ordained under the proposed change. Fortunately, after several months of discussion, the wording was changed to specifically state that local church ordinations would continue to be recognized and participated in by the other churches of our association. The new change was accepted and is now part of our association's constitution.

Certainly, those who wrote the original change had no malice in mind. They are all friends of mine who had been asked to make the language of our constitution congruent with national and state policy, but they could not see the change through the eyes of a bivocational pastor. They had not thought about what the language would say to those who serve in a bivocational capacity.

Fortunately, the American Baptist Churches/USA is now looking into ways the denomination can assist bivocational ministers. At a recent Ministers Council Senate meeting, a decision was made to develop a national bivocational ministry network. By using the American Baptist Personnel Services system, persons interested in bivocational ministry will be identified and contacted. Once the network is established, it will be a means of providing encouragement to bivocational ministers and churches. It will also enable the denomination to learn of the concerns and needs of those in bivocational ministry.

The Southern Baptist Convention offers support to its bivocational ministers and churches through the efforts of Dale Holloway, the National Missionary for Bivocational Ministries, and several bivocational consultants located throughout the denomination. In addition to his leadership and numerous speaking engagements, Holloway also edits a newsletter for bivocational ministers, *The Bivocational Beacon.*

Several Southern Baptist state conventions have bivocational fellowships that provide their ministers with support and recognition. Recently, a Baptist association in Texas called a consultant to work with their single-staff and bivocational churches. This individual is the first bivocational contract consultant to be paid by an association.[18]

Some denominations do not allow bivocational pastors to lead their churches. A pastor friend of mine from another denomination told me that his denomination does not permit its pastors to have outside jobs. Despite that policy, he knows of several pastors who do hold such jobs because their churches are simply too small to adequately provide for their pastors and their families. These jobs are kept secret from denominational leadership, and, perhaps in some cases, from the churches being served.

Such secrecy comes with a price. The pastor lives in fear that if his outside job is discovered he will be removed from his place of leadership. If the pastor's second job is discovered, his integrity will certainly be questioned and trust could be lost. At the same time, the church does not realize its pastor is experiencing financial problems, and therefore, does not address the problem.

Denominations will find it more difficult to attract and keep good ministers until they realize that such a policy may be driving good people out of ministry who desire to maintain their integrity while at the same time provide for their families. Among denominations that do permit bivocational pastors, many need to examine their policies regarding ordination and accreditation of their ministers. While high standards should be established for the ordination of ministers, a particular degree may not necessarily be the best way to evaluate whether an individual meets those standards. First Timothy 3:1–7 and Titus 1:5–9 provide the church with better ways to evaluate the spirituality of one who has been called into ministry. Those denominations whose policies do not welcome and affirm bivocational ministers will be sending these individuals, and the churches who called them, a message that their ministry is second-rate at best.

Every denomination should have a committee study the present and projected need for bivocational ministers in their churches. If the factors described above are occurring in the denomination, how is the denomination addressing them? If bivocational pastors are not acceptable to the denomination, where will their small churches find leadership in the future? If the denomination finds that it will have a need for bivocational pastors, how does it plan to help them prepare for ministry? Finally, how will the denomination validate the ministry of the bivocational pastor? These are difficult questions, but the time to answer them is now.

God has not been caught unaware by the factors described in this chapter. He is not a God of confusion and chaos, nor is he a God who wants his church to be without a shepherd. I believe he is now calling people to experience the joy of bivocational ministry.

THREE PROBLEM AREAS

George Barna has found that many ministers encounter frustration, discouragement, and a lack of fulfillment in their ministries.[1] To say that bivocational ministry is tough is not to say it is any more difficult than other types of ministry; however, there are some unique problems associated with bivocational ministry that must be addressed.

PROBLEM #1: A SECOND JOB

In addition to the demands of ministry, family, and personal needs, the bivocational minister will often spend as much as forty to fifty hours per week at a second job. Some bivocational pastors are fortunate enough to have a second job that involves only twenty hours per week, but they will still encounter the occasional conflict between their second job and their ministry. Funerals will need to be conducted during the day. Church members will be admitted to the hospital and will want to see their pastor. Training events, ministerial meetings, and denominational conferences will usually be held during the day, making it impossible for bivocational ministers to attend without missing work.

Some employers will be more lenient than others when these conflicts occur. Large companies, such as the one for which I worked, will have set policies concerning attendance that must be followed by all employees. Management cannot make exceptions for those who pastor a church, or they would have to make exceptions for all employees who have second jobs. If I had a funeral to conduct or a meeting I needed to attend, I usually took a vacation day.

It is important to maintain your integrity with your employer. Your employer is paying you to work for him not to witness to your fellow employees or to do other ministerial functions during the work day. Of course, every employer is different. The supervisors for whom I worked usually allowed us some freedom during our breaks, so I kept something handy to read. My tool cabinets always contained a Bible, magazines such as *Christianity Today* and *Leadership,* and at least one book about theology or ministry.

Bivocational ministers need to make sure they do not view their ministry as a godly calling and their second job as merely a means of paying the bills. As R. Kent Hughes reminds us, "There is no secular/sacred distinction, for all honest work done for the Lord is sacred."[2] Our work provides us with a powerful opportunity to be a witness both to our employers and to our fellow employees. Theologian Carl F. H. Henry wrote that the work of the Christian "ought not to be of such questionable caliber that it disgraces God, discredits one's employer, and affronts society."[3]

Hughes suggests several disciplines of work that every Christian should develop, including those of us in bivocational ministry. These are:

- energy—A Christian should not be a lazy employee (2 Thess. 3:6).
- enthusiasm—A Christian should work with enthusiasm regardless of whether the task is a prominent one or takes place behind the scenes (Col. 3:23).
- wholeheartedness—A Christian should work as if God were the employer (Eph. 6:5–8).
- excellence—A Christian should be committed to excellence in the workplace (Prov. 22:29).[4]

It is important to learn what your employer expects from the employees and then exceed those expectations. Since you know you will at times encounter conflicts between your job and your ministerial duties, talk to your employer about how best to resolve them before they become a problem. Your openness and honesty will be appreciated.

PROBLEM #2: IDENTITY PROBLEMS

A person will not be in bivocational ministry for long before someone calls him a part-time minister. If a bivocational pastor hears that label often enough and begins to believe it, he may develop some identity problems.[5] He may begin to doubt his call to ministry or question the validity of his ministry. The problem worsens when others begin expressing those same doubts.

I received a call from a search committee several years ago asking if I would be interested in becoming their pastor. The chair of the committee and I had a good discussion for several minutes, then she learned I was a bivocational pastor. She promptly informed me that their church, with an average attendance of sixty-five people on Sunday mornings, had been served by a full-time pastor for several years and that they "would not go backward by accepting a part-time pastor." As you might imagine, that comment did not sit well with me.

A bivocational pastor is not a part-time pastor. We are on call twenty-four hours a day just as any other pastor. We have sermons to prepare and deliver. We often teach Sunday school classes, sponsor youth groups, and lead music in our churches. We conduct funerals and weddings. We baptize new converts and lead the church in observing the Lord's Supper. If we do not have as many hospital visits to make or counseling sessions to conduct, it is only because the churches we lead usually have fewer people.

Never let the misconceptions others may have about your ministry cause you to question your call and your value to the work of the kingdom of God. The church you are serving as a bivocational pastor is probably a small church who needs the ministry you can provide. The members deserve quality ministry just as members of other churches, and you are able to provide that ministry to them. Praise God for the place he has called you to minister and for the ministry he has given you! Thank him for the impact your service can make on the lives of the members of your congregation. Hold your head up high as you realize that you are providing valuable ministry to God's family.

PROBLEM #3: JEALOUSY OF OTHER PASTORS

Unfortunately, some fully funded ministers are jealous of bivocational ministers.[6] While this jealousy may be due to several factors, it usually has to do with a bivocational pastor's financial situation.

A bivocational pastor is sometimes able to enjoy a higher standard of living than a fully supported pastor. This is especially true when the fully supported pastor is serving in a small church. The Southern Baptist Convention has more than seven thousand fully supported pastors now serving in churches with less than sixty people attending Sunday school each Sunday. Some of these pastors qualify for food stamps.[7] They and their families often struggle to make ends meet, so we should not be surprised if they become envious of a bivocational pastor whose family enjoys a higher standard of living.

Another area of potential jealousy involves security. Some pastors live in fear of offending the leaders of their church. They often live in the church parsonage and are dependent on the income from their church salary. A pastor told me once that he agreed with me on a particular point of doctrine, but he could not teach that viewpoint or he would be dismissed from his church. He had a wife and three children to consider.

Compare this pastor's situation to the freedom a bivocational pastor enjoys. If my church asked for my resignation tomorrow, I would still have other income by which I could support my family. We would still have a roof over our heads and food in our refrigerator. Our insurance would continue. Certainly, to be fired from my pastorate would have emotional consequences for my family and me. There would also be financial consequences, but we would not be as financially devastated as a fully supported pastor would be if he were dismissed from his church.

The fear of forced termination is real. One study found that 22.8 percent of the pastors in America have been forced to leave a ministry.[8] This same study found that one in four of these same individuals had been terminated more than once. It is not too difficult to understand why some pastors may be jealous of a bivocational pastor who is not completely dependent on a church for his family's financial well-being.

How does a bivocational pastor respond to a pastor who seems to be jealous of his financial security? First, understand where those feelings are coming from, and then respond to them in love. Certainly, a bivocational pastor does not want to brag about his financial situation or the security he finds in bivocational ministry. If God has chosen to bless you financially, you may be able to find ways to help your fellow pastor who is struggling to support his family. Your support and encouragement can go a long way in helping him overcome his fears and his feelings of jealousy.

PROBLEM #4: DIFFICULTY CHANGING CHURCHES

A bivocational pastor will find it difficult to change churches if he cannot move to another community. Being able to live in one place for several years is usually an advantage associated with bivocational ministry, but sometimes a pastor needs to move to another church. Such a move presents a problem with his second job and with area churches.

A church in our community contacted me about becoming its pastor. Although it is a much larger church than the one I serve and they offered a good salary package, the church was willing to let me remain bivocational. We had numerous talks, and I considered whether God was leading me to that church. In the end, I told them I was not interested in their pastorate.

I made that decision for many reasons. First, I was afraid my present church might be harmed if people followed me to my new church. I doubt many people would have followed me, but when a small church loses even a few people, it hurts the church. I was also concerned that former church members would contact me rather than their new pastor to conduct weddings or funerals or to visit people in the hospital. I felt there would be a potential for problems by pastoring another church in the same small community in which I live. Ultimately, the church who called me agreed.

Another factor that makes it difficult for a bivocational pastor to change churches is a lack of denominational leader support.[9] Although in my denomination ministers are not assigned to their places of service by denominational leaders, these leaders do play an important role as churches search for a new pastor. Leaders are usually contacted by ministers seeking a change of pastorate and by churches who need a new pastor, and their recommendations are important to both. Some bivocational pastors feel they have been discriminated against by the leaders of their denomination.

Some of this discrimination may be real, and it may be due to biases denominational leaders may have against bivocational ministry. I doubt, however, that much real bias actually exists. Bivocational pastors have proven themselves to be competent and effective ministers. At the same time, denominational leaders do need to consider the unique situation of a bivocational minister when deciding whether to recommend an individual to a church. Would this person be willing to move if that move would take him further from his other employment? Has this person taken advantage of educational opportunities to improve his ministry? Does this person have the gifts that would be required in a new place of service?

A bivocational pastor should discuss such issues with denominational leadership. Ask about additional training that would benefit your ministry. Discuss your goals and vision for ministry with your denominational support people. This information will enable them to better understand the type of ministry to which you have been called, and they will be more likely to include your name with their other recommendations. If you feel you are a victim of bias, talk to your denominational leaders and tell them of your feelings. Perhaps you are misreading them, or perhaps you will force them to confront biases they do have. Either way, an honest discussion will improve the situation.

Third, bivocational pastors may find it difficult to change churches because churches in their area are reluctant to call a pastor from a nearby church. You may be in a situation in which you feel a change of churches is necessary, but you also do not want to move to another community. Other churches in the area that would consider you may be concerned about damaging their relationship with the church you now serve.

As I mentioned earlier, this was a concern a church in our community had with me becoming their pastor. They did not want to hurt the relationship they had with my present church, and they did not want to hurt that church should people follow me to my new pastorate.

We had the same concern at Hebron several years ago when we decided to call a youth minister. A lay leader who was working with youth in another church in our association wanted a paid youth minister position. Some on our committee expressed a concern about whether our hiring him would offend the other church. I talked with some of the leaders of that church, and they assured me the church was supportive of his decision to seek a paid youth minister position. We decided to hire him, and our decision did not affect our relationship with the other church in a negative way.

A bivocational pastor needs to be aware that other churches in the area may be reluctant to consider him for their pastorate because of how it might affect their relationship with other churches in the community. Stealing sheep is bad enough, but stealing a shepherd may be a hanging offense!

PROBLEM #5: TIME CONSTRAINTS

Almost all pastors struggle with finding enough time to do everything they believe needs to be done.[10] The bivocational pastor has the additional time restraint of spending several hours each week in other employment. This problem is so critical that it will be addressed in detail in chapter 6, where I discuss the importance of maintaining a balance among the various activities that demand your time.

PROBLEM #6: LACK OF GROWTH IN THE CHURCH

Most bivocational churches are small, and for a number of reasons may remain small. Some of these reasons are:

- distance from population centers
- transient membership
- unknown denomination
- problematic history

Our society rewards growth, and church culture is no different. Walk into any Christian bookstore and you will see displays of books that explain how church growth should occur in every church. The popular speakers at seminars are those who have led their churches in tremendous growth. A pastor who serves a small church may well feel that he is less than an adequate leader because his church is not keeping up with the churches that are setting new attendance records each year.

This is unfortunate thinking. In the first place, when we think of church growth, we should not think of only numerical growth. We look at numerical growth because anyone can count nickels and noses, but what about the growth that occurs in the lives of the members of a church when they are served by a caring pastor who faithfully teaches them the Bible and points the way to Jesus Christ every week? Although it cannot be easily charted on a graph, isn't spiritual maturity more important than the number of visitors who attended a service on a particular Sunday?[11]

H. B. London and Neil B. Wiseman remind us that

> every assignment is holy ground because Jesus gave Himself for the people who live there. Every place is important because God wants you to accomplish something supernatural there. Every situation is special because ministry is needed there. Like Queen Esther, you have come to the Kingdom for a time like this.[12]

The bivocational pastor has to come to terms with the fact that he may never pastor the biggest church in the community, or else he is going to become miserable and frustrated. He must not allow others to define ministerial success for him and his church. Instead, he needs to clearly understand what God's call is to him and his church at this particular time in history. Success will occur when he has fulfilled that call.

HOW DOES THE BIVOCATIONAL MINISTER DEAL WITH THESE PROBLEMS?

The most important thing any pastor can do is to be certain of his calling into the ministry. A person who simply chooses ministry as a vocation is going to find it difficult to survive the problems he will encounter. Early in my ministry I read that no person should choose ministry if he could be happy doing anything else. Only those who have been called by God to serve as ministers will be able to stand when ministry gets tough. J. H. Jowett once wrote, "Now I hold with profound conviction that before a man selects the Christian ministry as his vocation he must have the assurance that the selection has been imperatively constrained by the eternal God."[13]

All pastors need to be certain of their calling into the ministry because that calling will be questioned several times during the course of their service. Ordination councils will ask them to describe their call to the ministry, and most pastoral selection committees will ask the same question.

This is not an easy question to answer. God often calls his ministers in that still, small voice that is heard only in a person's spirit. Seldom are there outward signs to confirm such a calling. For most people, like myself, there is simply an inner assurance that God has called them to the ministry. Even though it is difficult to put into words, such a calling strengthens a minister and enables him to withstand the problems that arise in ministry.

The bivocational pastor also needs to be sure he has been called into a *pastoral* ministry. A number of my friends who have served as bivocational ministers served in capacities other than the pastorate. Ephesians 4:11 tells us that "[God] gave some to be apostles, some prophets, some evangelists, and some pastors and teachers." All of these ministers are given to the church for the same reason—to equip the church for the work of ministry.

Doran C. McCarty correctly points out that God's call to ministry is developmental.[14] As our gifts and skills change, God's call on our lives may change as well. His initial call may be to bivocational ministry, but that call may later change to a fully funded position. We may begin in a pastoral ministry and later find ourselves being called to a teaching or administrative ministry. As bivocational ministers, we may find God calling us to start a new church. It is important that we not consider God's call to be one that never changes. We must keep evaluating God's call on our lives and stay sensitive to the possibility that his calling may lead us into different areas of ministry as we mature and develop new abilities.

The important thing is to use the gifts God has given you. If he has gifted you to be a pastor and called you to that ministry, then follow that call. Bivocational ministry is tough enough without trying to minister in areas in which you have not been gifted and called.

One of my friends served for many years as a bivocational evangelist. He led a number of revivals and saw many people come to Christ as a result of his ministry. After a number of years serving as an evangelist, he saw his gifts begin to change and accepted the pastorate of a church in his community.

Another friend, who worked in the same factory in which I worked, has served for many years as a teacher. Not only does he teach in his own church, but he travels around to other churches and teaches the Word of God. He has taken groups of people to Mexico to minister to churches there. While he has served for many years in this capacity, he has never felt God's leading to become a pastor.

When you follow God's leading and exercise the gifts he has given you, you will find bivocational ministry to be exciting, challenging, and rewarding, despite the problems you will face.

FOUR PREPARATION FOR BIVOCATIONAL MINISTRY

Over the past several years, I have known a number of bivocational ministers. Some have been successful, but a number of others are no longer in the ministry. Although this is a generalization, the ones who have remained in the ministry and been successful are those who realized that bivocational ministry deserved their best effort.

Ministry is tough. Pastors today face issues that our predecessors never encountered. AIDS, single parenthood, abortion, welfare dependency, widespread violence among the young, racial problems, and values clarification are just some of the difficult issues that must be addressed by today's pastor. I cannot imagine hearing one of the pastors of my youth talk about condoms in a sermon, but I have referred to condoms and the myth of safe sex in numerous messages.

How does the church minister to a twenty-nine-year-old grandmother? Perhaps even more important, what can the church do to prevent more twenty-nine-year-old grandmothers?[1] How does a church minister to single adults, many of whom are divorced, most of whom do not attend church?[2] How should the church respond when new believers want to leave their AIDS-infected baby in the church nursery? How can the church minister to the young woman who has had an abortion or several abortions? These are just a few of the issues that make ministry today so difficult.

Another problem affecting the way we do ministry is the way people today relate to churches. Baby boomers and their offspring (busters) often look at church in a much different way than did their parents and grandparents. Many boomers and busters are more apt to attend a particular church because of its style of worship rather than its denominational label. Some will regularly attend two or more churches because of the different ministries the churches offer.[3] Even among those who regularly attend just one church, many are less likely to become members of that church.[4] As one individual told me, "I want to be known as a Christian, a follower of Christ, not a Baptist." Churches who require membership before an individual is allowed to serve in the church may discover it is difficult to find enough members to fill all the positions in the church.

People today also tend to have much higher expectations of the churches they attend. The malls where they shop have paved parking; they expect their church to have paved parking as well. They own the finest stereo equipment available on the market; they are not going to be pleased with a church piano that is out of tune. This computer generation is also not going to be too impressed with flannel boards and mimeograph machines. Parents will not accept a church nursery that is located behind the furnace room and staffed by two teenage girls.[5]

The bivocational pastor should see these changes taking place in the church as opportunities for ministry, and he should see that proper ministry in such circumstances will require his best efforts. The bivocational pastor, therefore, needs basic training and then an ongoing program of study to minister in our changing times.

There is no calling greater than the one God gives when he calls a person to pastoral ministry. We have an obligation to prepare ourselves and to fulfill that call to the best of our abilities.

WHAT ABOUT SEMINARY?

Until recent years, it was widely assumed that a pastor needed a seminary education to be prepared to minister in a church. Because many seminaries now seem more interested in being graduate schools of theology rather than places to prepare for pastoral ministry, a number of people have challenged this assumption.[6] Leith Anderson writes that "traditional seminary education is designed to train research theologians, who are to become parish practitioners. Probably they are adequately equipped for neither."[7]

Many seminary graduates agree. In a study of over one thousand pastors, only one out of four said he was very well prepared by his seminary training for the tasks of pastoring.[8]

Bivocational pastors would have a difficult time attending seminary anyway. Many do not have the college degree required for entrance into a seminary. Pastoring a church and working does not lend itself very well to the study and classroom attendance required by traditional seminary education. Unfortunately, because of the types of problems mentioned above, a bivocational pastor, not unlike a fully supported pastor, needs all the training he can get in order to best serve his church. Where will he find the training he needs?

MY EXPERIENCE

I became the pastor at Hebron with no ministerial experience or seminary training. Frankly, I was not very interested in seminary. This was at a time when the seminary closest to our area was dealing with liberalism on campus. I had met a few graduates of that institution who rejected much of what the Bible teaches, and were, in fact, teaching what I believed to be error. I wanted no part of that.

However, several months after I began my ministry, God began to show me some areas of ministry in which I was rather weak. I began to understand that if I was to be the minister God had called me to be, I needed to strengthen those weak areas. God calls us to ministry, empowers us to do ministry, and gives us the gifts that enable us to minister, but we have the responsibility to hone those gifts if we wish to reach our greatest potential as a minister of God.

I had two problems to overcome. One, I was not a college graduate. Two, I worked the day shift in a factory fifty miles north of my home. Of course, there are no problems God cannot solve when we are committed to doing what he has called us to do.

I became aware of Boyce Bible School, which is a part of the Southern Baptist Theological Seminary in Louisville, Kentucky. Boyce was established to provide ministry training to people just like me: people called to ministry later in life and who do not have a college education.

Unfortunately, Boyce offers classes only during the morning hours. My workplace is fifty miles north of my home, and Boyce is fifty miles south of where I live. After a long talk with my wife and the church, I decided to transfer to the midnight shift and attend classes during the day. Every day that I attended class I had a two-hundred-mile commute from my home to work, from work to school, and then back home after classes. Most semesters I limited my classes to two or three days, so while Boyce offers a two-year program, it took me four years to complete my classes and earn a degree in Christian ministry.

I did not stop my formal education with that diploma. Also about fifty miles south of my house is a university that accepted many of the credits I earned at Boyce. Each semester they offer a number of classes in my community, so I had to take only some of the classes on campus. I transferred my credits and began work on a bachelor's degree. Seven years later I graduated with a bachelor's degree in general studies. By enrolling in the general studies program, I did not have to declare a major, which allowed me to take more classes that I felt would benefit me in the ministry. I took a number of classes in psychology, sociology, communication, and business.

It was not easy spending those years in school, but I believe that I grew as an individual, and I believe that my ministry benefited as well. At Boyce Bible School I learned more about theology, but I also learned the practical skills I need to minister as a pastor. My university courses helped me better understand people, and they also enabled me to be a more educated person who can better relate to others.

College courses may be affordable for a bivocational minister because a secular employer may be willing to pay for them. Many companies, especially larger ones, have tuition assistance programs available for their employees. At the end of each semester I spent at the university, Cummins Engine Company reimbursed me for my tuition expenses. My classes at Boyce Bible School did not qualify for their program, but every class I took at the university did qualify because it made me a more valuable employee to Cummins. If you are interested in taking college courses, talk to the human resource director, your manager, or the owner of your company.

HOW CAN YOU PREPARE FOR BIVOCATIONAL MINISTRY?

Formal Education

A number of seminaries now have schools similar to Boyce Bible School that attempt to teach pastors the practical skills they will need to serve their churches. Some of these skills include sermon preparation and delivery, church administration, pastoral care, leadership, and the use of proper English grammar. Don't laugh! I consider the two English grammar classes at Boyce to be among the most important classes I have ever taken. Of course, these schools also offer theology classes, church history classes, and classes that study individual books of the Bible.

A number of factors may make it impossible for a bivocational pastor to attend classes at a school, but other options are available. The Southern Baptist Convention offers Seminary Extension classes that allow individuals to take many of these same courses at home. Personally, I tried to take some Seminary Extension courses and found that I did not have the discipline to complete them at home. However, many have completed their studies through Seminary Extension and found it to be an excellent program.

Several schools now offer seminary studies by correspondence. Although some of these programs are excellent, one must be careful not to enroll with a diploma mill. Anyone can earn meaningless degrees to hang on their walls, but neither God, the members of the church, nor an individual's peers will be impressed with such a degree. Hopefully, you are interested in learning skills that will help you to be a better minister. Earning a degree should be a secondary concern to the bivocational pastor who desires to be prepared to minister in these difficult times.

One new approach to education that some bivocational ministers may find appealing is the option of studying on-line. Major seminaries such as Fuller, Bethel, and Trinity International offer on-line programs ranging from bachelor's degrees to doctorates.[9] Some Bible colleges also offer classes via the Internet, and the list of schools recognizing the need for such education is growing. The advantages to students are that they don't have to spend time driving to classes and they can do their studies at times that are convenient to them. Drawbacks to correspondence classes include a lack of interaction between students and teachers and the length of time it takes to receive graded tests. On-line studies should improve both of these problems.

Continuing Education

Many professional people realize that the basic education they received to prepare them for their chosen work is not adequate for our changing times. Doctors, dentists, attorneys, engineers, teachers, and other professional people are required to take a certain number of continuing education courses each year. In the company that my family owns, the service technician who holds the master's license for our company is required to complete ten hours of classroom study each year before he can renew that license. If a service technician is required to take regular continuing education classes each year, how much more important is it that those of us in ministry regularly attend seminars and other continuing study opportunities?

A bivocational pastor may be wondering, "How can I attend a seminar when I can't find the time to do everything else I need to do?" I have wondered the same thing myself. However, this question demonstrates an incomplete understanding of ministry. Jesus demonstrated in his own ministry the value of making time for refreshing and personal renewal. I am not suggesting he attended seminars, but he did leave his ministry for times of prayer and rest.

Ministry does not consist only of doing. Preparation is also a part of ministry. We will be much more effective as pastors when we learn that personal renewal and times of preparation enable us to meet the challenges we will experience in ministry. Continuing education is an important part of that preparation.

Every church should provide money in its budget for continuing education for its pastor. That money should carry over at least one year if it is not used so that it remains available to the pastor. The pastor's job description should specify how many days each year the pastor is allowed to be away from the church for continuing education studies. The pastor and the church both benefit when this is done.

I have attended seminars on church conflict, evangelism, church growth, and reaching out to inactive members. The church paid for me to attend these seminars, but the benefit the church received far outweighed their investment.

Denominational Workshops

Most denominations offer various workshops during the year that are helpful to a bivocational minister and his church. These workshops are usually free of charge. Quite often, they are offered by a regional association, so they are tailored to the specific needs of an area. Many denominational leaders will even develop a specific workshop to address common problems their pastors are facing. You only need to let them know what these problems are.

A common complaint about denominational workshops is that they are not held at times convenient for bivocational ministers. There is no question that denominations need to do a better job of meeting the training needs of their bivocational ministers who have to juggle ministry with work schedules.[10] However, it is also true that it is impossible for denominational planners to plan every meeting at a time that is convenient for every bivocational minister.[11] We need to accept the fact that we will not be able to attend every workshop offered by our denomination. It is our responsibility to pick the workshops that address the areas of ministry in which we are the weakest and make the time to attend them.

Training Offered by Your Employer

Another resource that can help you prepare for ministry is one many people do not think about: the training opportunities offered by your employer. The company I worked for offered many types of training to their employees, and I took advantage of nearly every one for which I qualified. Although I was a shop employee, my last job required extensive use of a computer. Not only did my company pay for the cost of my computer training, it also paid my wages while I was taking the course and my mileage to and from the training site. The course taught me how to use the software programs used in our company. Guess what kind of software I bought for my personal computer? That's right—the same software for which I received training through my employer. When your employer offers training that will help you in your job, keep in mind how you can also use it to assist you in your ministry.

Reading Is Essential

Another ingredient necessary in preparing for bivocational ministry is reading. Most successful bivocational pastors I have known have been avid readers. My personal library is an essential part of my ministry. Theology books and commentaries are necessary for sermon preparation and teaching. Books on pastoral ministry, church growth, evangelism, and counseling help me provide pastoral ministry and leadership to our church. Books on the Christian life inspire, challenge, and motivate me to live a life that is pleasing to God. I also receive some Christian periodicals and two weekly fax letters from Christian organizations to help me stay current on events that affect the church.

W. A. Criswell is correct when he writes, "No man can meet the demands of a pulpit who does not constantly and earnestly study."[12] He strongly encourages pastors to keep their libraries in their homes so they can study without the interruptions that so often occur in church offices.[13] This is certainly good advice for the bivocational minister who may need to study early in the morning or late at night.

Of course, we are not to read simply to prepare sermons. Alexandr Solzhenitsyn reminds us that "the meaning of earthly existence lies not, as we have grown used to thinking, in prospering but in the development of the soul."[14] This is certainly true of pastors. Before we were called to the ministry, we were first called to grow spiritually. A pastor can hide a lack of spiritual growth in his life for a period of time through hard work, but such superficial success will eventually take its toll on his personal life and ministry. H. B. London and Neil B. Wiseman write, "Personal spiritual growth is absolutely essential for a pastor if he wants to enjoy *sustained* satisfactions and beneficial ministry" (emphasis added).[15]

Reading, especially devotional reading, is an important tool in that spiritual development. Richard J. Foster writes of the importance of reading:

> The purpose of the Spiritual Disciplines is the total transformation of the person. They aim at replacing old destructive habits

of thought with new life-giving habits. Nowhere is this purpose more clearly seen than in the Discipline of study. The apostle Paul tells us that we are transformed through the renewal of the mind (Romans 12:2).[16]

Along with the Bible, Foster lists some Christian classics that should be read and studied to help in our spiritual development. A few of these are *Mere Christianity* by C. S. Lewis, *The Imitation of Christ* by Thomas à Kempis, and *The Cost of Discipleship* by Dietrich Bonhoeffer.[17]

You will never retain everything you read, so it is important to develop a filing system to store information for later retrieval. Some pastors number their books on the outside edge similar to the way in which a library numbers its books. They may use the Dewey Decimal System or develop their own numbering system.

One pastor I know records helpful information and page numbers on the blank page found at the end of most books. When he finishes reading a book, that information is entered into his computer filing system. It may look something like this: church unity 422:102ff. The "422" represents the number he assigned to the book, and "102ff." refers to the page numbers containing the pertinent information. The next time he writes a sermon on church unity, he has useful information at his fingertips. He files magazine articles, newspaper stories, and mailings in a similar way. He removes an article from a magazine and writes a number in the upper right-hand corner, then he lists that number and the title of the article in his computer system. The articles are filed in numerical order with fifty items per file.

This system would not work for everyone, and I am certain there are better systems available. But it does work for some, and that is all that really matters. You need to find a system that works for you so you can enjoy the full benefit of your reading. When you are looking for information for a sermon or to share with a group in your church, you will be glad you took the time to organize the information in a way that allows you to access it easily.

I recommend that churches provide a certain amount of money in their budgets for a book allowance. Books and subscriptions are expensive, and their cost should not be borne by the pastor alone. A church benefits when its pastor reads and studies good material, so the church should be willing to help pay for that material.

A pastor needs to read more than just church-related material. Reading a wide variety of material gives a pastor additional insights into life and the needs of people. I am fascinated by the Watergate incident that occurred during President Nixon's term of office, and I have most of the books written by those who were involved in it. Many of my sermon illustrations have come from reading about that event. I also have a number of books that deal with management, sales, personal finance, and sports. While most students sold their textbooks back to the school, I kept mine to use as reference books.

Again, you may be thinking, "Where can I find the time to read books not directly related to sermon preparation?" Let me give you some suggestions that help me.

I always keep a book in my truck. If I am in a line at a bank or tied up in traffic, I read a few pages while I am waiting. I go to a gym several days each week to exercise. Part of my workout involves a thirty-minute walk on a treadmill. While walking, I can read a chapter or two. I never go to the doctor's office without a book to read in the waiting room. Finally, knowing how important reading is to my ministry, I simply make time to read. We can always find the time to do those things we truly believe are important.

There is no question that ministry today is demanding. Pastors face many challenges that previous generations did not have to face. Bivocational pastors usually face those challenges with less formal education, training, and resources, but that does not mean they are doomed to be defeated. This chapter outlines a number of steps the bivocational pastor can take to better prepare himself for the challenges he will face in ministry. Be honest with yourself and admit those areas of weakness in your ministry, and then find ways to strengthen those areas. When you do, you will be ready for every challenge that confronts your ministry.

FIVE A REWARDING MINISTRY

So far this book has dealt with problems and potential difficulties associated with bivocational ministry. By now you may be wondering when the discussion is going to focus on the *joy* of bivocational ministry. Your patience is about to be rewarded.

Most people want their life's work to count for something. Those who feel called by God to serve him in a church ministry want to believe their ministry has significance. Can bivocational ministry be rewarding both to the minister and to the church being served? The answer to that question is a resounding yes!

Leon Wilson believes that bivocational ministry is essential if churches want to reach rural and urban communities. He should know. As a bivocational pastor, he started South Park Baptist Church in Oklahoma City in 1979 and led that church as it grew to a 550-member congregation.[1] Although this may not be normal church growth for most bivocational churches, Pastor Wilson's experience shows us just how effective and rewarding bivocational ministry can be.

I want to spend the next few pages discussing some of the rewards and joys I have experienced in bivocational ministry. Looking back over my eighteen years of ministry at Hebron Baptist Church, I am amazed at how far God has brought us and how he has blessed us. For every good thing that will be described in this chapter, God deserves all the glory. I went to the church with no experience, no education, and no idea of what I would do. I had only a desire to fulfill what I believed was God's call on my life to be a pastor. I have often told people that my greatest contribution to the blessings our church has received is that I have stayed for a while and encouraged the people to trust God to do some great things in their lives.

HEBRON BAPTIST CHURCH IN 1981

Hebron Baptist Church was once a strong church with a significant ministry in the rural community in which it is located. The community was forever changed, however, when the army purchased most of its land for a munition testing facility. Many in the church sold their farms to the army and moved away. Church attendance dropped to a third of what it once was. A long succession of short-term pastors, usually students, compounded the church's problems.

The church developed two conditions that are typical of churches in such situations. First, the remaining members began to see themselves as less than a normal church.[2] Second, along with the series of short-term pastors came a reluctance to attempt new programs. Church members believed that pastors who proposed new programs would not stay long enough to see them through to completion.[3] These two conditions led to apathy in the church, which made effective ministry difficult to achieve.

When I began my ministry in this church in 1981, the church was experiencing other problems as well. Budget requirements were minimal, but the church was not meeting them. Sunday school and the Sunday morning worship service were the church's only forms of ministry. The former pastor had submitted his resignation just minutes prior to being asked to do so, and two families had left that same Sunday. There was a great deal of pain and discouragement in the church.

FIRST STEPS

We took some fairly simple first steps after my arrival. A member agreed to lead a youth group for the few young people who attended the church. Some members expressed an interest in starting a Sunday evening worship service, so we began one a few weeks later. New programs were not what was needed most at that time, however. The people needed to know they were loved and appreciated. At the beginning of my ministry, most of my time was spent visiting the members of the church and trying to learn what they needed and what they believed the church needed.

Many people had been deeply hurt and had left the church in previous years. Therefore, I also spent a good deal of time visiting those who no longer attended the church. Although only a few returned to the church, and only for a short time, I felt good about my attempt as the new pastor to reach out to them.

Every pastor needs a period of time at the beginning of a new ministry to learn about the church and the people. In a small church, especially one that has had problems, a pastor may need a rather lengthy period of time to accomplish this task. Some believe that it takes about five years to lay the foundation for an effective ministry in a small church.[4] When the average pastorate is less than five years, should we be surprised that so many churches struggle to develop an effective ministry in their communities?

FIRST CHALLENGES

After I had been at Hebron for a couple of years, we began to discuss some of the needs associated with the building. Our sanctuary had been built in 1906, and an education wing had been added in the early 1970s. The floor of the sanctuary was wood with only a carpet runner down the center aisle. The wood floor was quite noisy when people walked on it, and it needed a good cleaning. The pews were beautifully curved, but they were also old and in desperate need of a cleaning, and many people did not find them very comfortable. The sanctuary had not been painted in years.

While we were discussing what needed to be done first, the decision was made for us. Following a worship service one hot summer morning, I noticed that a visitor's white shirt stuck to the back of the pew as he tried to get up. To make matters even worse, the varnish on the pew had come off on his shirt. We never saw that visitor again! Shortly after this occurred, we voted to cover the pews with padding and cloth at a cost of $2,236.00

Although the finances of the church were more stable now, we still did not have that much money available. We decided we would not do the work until we raised the full amount. A money thermometer like those found in many small churches was used to show our progress as we attempted to raise the money we needed. Within a few months, the money was there, and we proceeded with the work.

That was the first time the church had raised money for a specific purpose in several years. The fact that members were willing to do so said something about how they were beginning to feel about the church and themselves. It was a tremendous victory for the church.

The next year we did the same thing in order to paint the sanctuary and install wall-to-wall carpeting in the sanctuary. Again, the people gave to this special need, and the work was done without borrowing money. Before the year was out, the church also paid my expenses for a mission trip to Haiti. Expenditures in 1985 were a record high for the church.

All this set the stage for the next big event in the life of the church. In 1986, the American Baptist Churches started a mission program called Alive in Mission. This program was to raise money to begin new church development and to increase the number of missionaries we could send overseas. Individuals could donate money or they could sign a three-year pledge if they wished to give a larger amount. The denomination challenged each church with a goal that was based on a formula that included past mission giving. Our church's goal was $3,283.00, which we voted to accept. A few people questioned whether that goal was too high for us to reach, but when the fund-raising drive was completed, the members of Hebron Baptist Church had pledged a total of $11,100.00!

This was an unbelievable amount of money for a church that only five years earlier had struggled financially, but this was not the same church. Yes, many of the people were the same, but their attitude was much different. They had experienced victories as a church when they raised money for the improvements to the facility. They had confidence that they could do great things for God despite the size of the church.

Each year the American Baptist Churches of Indiana recognizes various churches, based on average attendance, as the church of the year. I was so overjoyed with what our church had accomplished that I submitted the church's name for consideration. A few months later I received a letter stating that we had been selected for that honor. The following Sunday I wept as I read the letter to the church. We had much to celebrate for God had done marvelous things in our congregation. At the state convention that fall, we received our recognition and a plaque stating that we were the church of the year. Our local newspaper ran a front-page story about our achievements and recognition.

THE WORK AND THE BLESSINGS CONTINUE

The church continued to spend money to improve our facility and the ministries we offered. Four of the most unusual purchases we made, especially for a small church such as ours, were television commercials that we could run on our local cable. These professionally made commercials created such a positive response from area people that we purchased three more the following year. They were broadcast into approximately seven thousand homes each day.

Since cable coverage does not extend into much of the rural community, we began searching for a way to reach out to that area. In 1992, we voted to mail a twelve-page newspaper to three thousand rural homes each quarter. This paper, published and mailed in Georgia, includes excellent articles about families and Christian living. After almost every issue, I hear positive comments from someone who has received it.

Many other exciting things happened in 1992. A new nursery was started with funds donated for that purpose. A ramp was installed that allowed easier access into the facility by those with physical limitations. The church doubled its mission support over 1991 totals. Eleven people were baptized into the church. A member started and led a home Bible study. The youth program was reactivated.

As a result of these activities, the church once again received the award for church of the year. Again, I read the letter to the church with tears in my eyes. What wonderful things God had done in and through the church! These activities had not been pastor-driven. While I had suggested some of them, the members of the church had made them happen. They had used the gifts God had given them to achieve wonderful things for his glory.

CURRENT BLESSINGS

Due to the location of our church, it will probably never be a large church. We now average fifty people at our morning worship service. Of course, few people who attended the church when I first came here as pastor are still here. The average age is certainly much younger than in 1981, and there are more children, which bodes well for the future of the church.

Nineteen ninety-six was another wonderful year with many achievements for the church. We saw a slight increase in attendance at all our services. Offerings averaged about $150.00 per week above our budget requirements. We were able to increase our mission giving 38 percent over 1995. This enabled us to have the highest per capita giving to United Missions in our area with nearly $180.00 per person. That per capita giving was the second highest in the state.

Our increase in mission giving resulted from a decision we made a few years earlier to increase the percentage of our budget given to missions. Initially, we gave 10 percent of our weekly offering to our denomination's United Mission. We decided to increase that by 1 percent per year until we reached 15 percent. In 1996, we were giving 13 percent of our offerings to United Mission. With our offerings as high as they were, our mission giving increased substantially as well.

One important factor that led to an increase in mission support was a mission trip I took to Haiti. A group of men from Indiana went to Cap Haitian to work on a youth center that had been damaged by fire. We also spent time visiting some of our denomination's missions in the surrounding area. One afternoon we visited the home of our director of missions in Haiti, which gave us a better understanding of how he lives and works.

Naturally, all my experiences were shared with my church when I returned. I created a slide presentation that was given at Hebron and at some other churches as well. References to that trip still occasionally appear in my sermons. That trip excited me about mission work, and our church has caught that excitement. People give money to those things in which they believe and that excite them.

Being bivocational does not mean you cannot participate in such experiences as a mission trip. In fact, a hands-on experience such as this may be especially helpful for one who has had limited opportunities to study mission work. You may have to invest some vacation time, but that is a small price to pay for such a growth opportunity. Visionaries in your church will see the value of providing you with the time and the finances to participate in a mission trip. Such a trip does not even need to be overseas to be beneficial for your own personal spiritual development and for increasing mission awareness in your church.

At the time of this writing in 1999, our offerings average about $500.00 above our budget requirements, and we are giving 15 percent of those offerings to United Mission. Last year we baptized twelve people and saw twenty new members join our church. Five people have been baptized so far this year. We have increased the size of our parking area and added additional seating in our sanctuary. Our church is trying to purchase some adjacent land so we can build a new fellowship area. Attendance remains strong, and some wonderful things are happening in people's lives.

Can a bivocational pastor have an effective ministry? I have found my years at Hebron to be exceedingly rewarding and challenging. Significant ministry has occurred here in the past eighteen years, and I will repeat what I said earlier in this chapter: Much of my contribution has simply involved staying at the church for a number of years and giving the members the freedom to exercise their gifts for ministry. I see my role as that of a teacher, an encourager, and an enabler.

INVOLVEMENT OF THE LAITY

Our church has accomplished the things it has because the laypeople have become more involved. They understand it is impossible for me to do all the work of ministry. Even in large churches, with fully supported pastors, it is not possible for a pastor or staff to provide all the ministry needed in the church. The demands are simply too great.

Most people in most churches receive good crisis care from their pastor, but few receive adequate ongoing pastoral care. By the time the pastor spends time with the sick, the hospitalized, the grieving, the confused, and the angry, there is little time to visit those members who do not have an immediate problem. There are not many churches, if any, that could financially afford sufficient pastoral staff to take care of all the ministry needs in the church. Laypeople, when properly encouraged and trained, can provide much of the ongoing care needed in a church.[5]

Of course, Paul teaches in Ephesians 4 that the work of the minister is to equip church members to do the work of ministry. The Bible says nothing about a church in which the ordained minister does all the work while the church members sit on the sidelines watching, either cheering or criticizing. A pastor's primary role is to challenge, encourage, and train the members to do the work of ministry for which God has gifted them.

The bivocational pastor has a unique opportunity to model that type of ministry to his church. When the pastor goes to a second job, it is much more difficult to put him up on a pedestal as one who is different and more specially equipped to serve God. As I often explain to my congregation, God has given me certain gifts to be used in ministry. My gifts may not be your gifts, and my ministry may not be your ministry, but you also have gifts and a ministry that God has given you. I then encourage them to discover those gifts and find ways to use them in serving God. Their responses to that challenge have led our church to accomplish some wonderful things.

In churches large and small, laypeople are the ones who introduce special ministries to their churches. They see the need, they develop a program to meet that need, and they provide leadership for that program. Saddleback Valley Community Church, with over ten thousand people attending worship services each week, has numerous programs to provide ministry to its community. However, the church's staff does not begin any new ministry. Their ministries begin when someone comes with a vision for a new ministry and the willingness to lead it.[6] George G. Hunter III calls this the rise of the entrepreneurial laity, and he sees this as a vital part of a ministering church.[7]

PERSONAL REWARDS

Bivocational ministry is also personally rewarding to the pastor. People in a bivocational church often have different expectations of their pastor than do those in a church led by a fully funded pastor. At one time we were having a Wednesday night Bible study in my home each week. My daughter played basketball for her junior high school team, and their awards banquet was going to be held on a Wednesday night. I mentioned this to the Bible study group, and they insisted that we not meet the next week so I could attend her banquet. They appreciated our family and respected the fact that I wanted to support my daughter in this activity. Some of my fully funded pastor friends have told me that their churches expect them to be at every service unless they are on vacation or are ill. They would not be permitted to miss a church event to attend a child's activity.

When our son entered high school, my wife noticed that he seemed bothered by something. He was a good student, popular, and involved in the basketball and baseball programs at school. We finally learned that he was concerned I would take a position at another church and we would move from the area before he completed high school. My wife and I discussed it, prayed about it, and I made the commitment to him that I would not move from the area until he finished high school. His immediate relief was evident.

As a fully supported pastor, that might have been a dangerous promise to make. In three years, anything can happen in a church that would make it necessary for the pastor to move to another place of ministry. I would not have to move even if my ministry at Hebron ended. I could simply remain at my second job until our son graduated and then consider going back into the ministry after my promise to him had been fulfilled. I have always found that sense of independence to be a rewarding part of bivocational ministry.

THESE BLESSINGS CAN BE EXPERIENCED BY ANY CHURCH AND PASTOR

The Bible tells us that God is no respecter of persons. What he has done in our church, he can do in any church. In fact, he wants to do even greater things if we will allow him to do so. If churches shifted their focus from their problems to what God wants to do in them and through them, we would begin to experience a revival in our churches that would change entire communities.

I am convinced that it is only when a pastor stays at a church long enough and truly becomes a part of the congregation that effective ministry can happen. It is then that people's lives can be touched and changed by the power of God. It is then that the church can begin to see beyond its problems and begin to see a vision of the ministry God has for them. Then they can experience the kinds of victories that will cause them to get excited about the work of the kingdom of God. This excitement will lead them to see others through the eyes of God, helping them to develop greater compassion for others. That compassion will cause people outside the church to be attracted to what God is doing in the church. When God's love, flowing through your congregation, begins to touch the hearts of those outside the church, many will turn to Christ. The church will grow as people are brought to a saving relationship with the Lord Jesus Christ. During this entire process, you as the pastor have the privilege of experiencing the joy of bivocational ministry.

SIX THE NEED FOR BALANCE

He had been the pastor of the same church in a southern state for thirty years, but now he was retired from pastoral ministry and teaching a class at Boyce Bible School. We learned a lot from him that semester, but we learned the most important lesson the day he stood before us with tears in his eyes and talked about his first wife.

The demands of pastoral ministry had required most of his time. As he neared retirement, however, he and his wife had made plans to travel the country and try to make up for the time they had not been able to spend together. A few months before his retirement, his wife became ill and died. His voice was gentle as always, but his tears showed the emotion he was feeling as he told us not to assume we will always have the time to do later what we want to do. Later may not come. He urged us to spend time now with our families and do the things that will provide us with wonderful memories. We do not have the promise of tomorrow, so we must make today count.

BALANCE IS REQUIRED

Ministry is difficult and demanding. To fulfill God's call on our lives requires us to give the best of our time and effort. This isn't always easy. We are often pulled in many different directions. It takes time to minister to those with personal and family problems. It takes time to prepare biblical sermons that bring honor to God and speak to his people. It takes time to handle the administrative tasks of the church. It takes time to provide leadership to the various committees and boards.

Time is a precious commodity in everyone's life. We each have 168 hours a week to use. No more, no less. Every minute we spend on one activity is lost for another activity. Each of us must decide how we want to use every hour of every day of our lives. If we fail to make that decision, we will find that much of our time has been wasted.

I had another professor at Boyce whom I admired a great deal. I enrolled in every class he taught because of the practical wisdom he brought to the classroom. He had a saying he often repeated: You get done what you spend time doing.

If I had a nickel for every time I have repeated that to someone, I could retire to my own island. I have printed that phrase and posted it above my desk, and it has become an important part of my philosophy of life and work. That statement has been included in sermons and church leadership discussions and shared with non-church audiences as well.

Another statement that contains great truth is this: If you do not control your time, someone else will. You have to take control of your calendar, or other people will control your life. You will find yourself constantly working on other people's agendas rather than your own. Someone has slightly altered a Campus Crusade for Christ statement to read, God loves you, and everyone else has a wonderful plan for your life!

Every pastor, including bivocational pastors, must set priorities for the use of their time. We must control our calendars, or our lives and ministries may become unbalanced with serious consequences for many people. You get done what you spend time doing. Along with balancing time, we must also maintain balance in the expectations we have for our ministries, our churches, and our families. Every pastor should heed the words of Romans 12:3: "For I say, through the grace given to me, to everyone who is among you, not to think of himself more highly than he ought to think, but to think soberly, as God has dealt to each one a measure of faith."

Jesus taught and modeled servant-leadership, and pastors would be wise to follow his example. We are not the head of our churches, Christ is (Eph. 5:23). Yes, there will be times when the church does not respond as we think it should to our leadership, and those times can be frustrating. We must remember, however, that we have been called to serve and lead, not demand and push. If we forget this, our ministry to our churches will be out of balance, which can have tragic consequences.

What are your expectations for your family? What expectations does your church have for your family? The families of pastors often feel as if they live in a glass house with everyone watching. Ministering in such an environment is not spiritually or emotionally healthy for a family. Without balance in this area of family life, ministry will be a chore and potentially harmful to our families.

The remainder of the chapter explores how to balance the demands on our time and how to balance expectations. I encourage you to read this chapter slowly and prayerfully. How well you are able to maintain balance in these areas of your life will greatly determine how successful, satisfying, and joy-filled your ministry will be.

Work

It is difficult to write a section on balancing work, because the types of second jobs bivocational ministers have are so varied. When I worked in a factory, I was expected to be there forty hours every week, except for vacations and sick days. I had to schedule everything else around that forty-hour work week. Now, as a small business owner, my hours are more flexible, but the responsibilities are much greater. A person who is working on commission may find himself working odd hours. He may work many hours one week and fewer hours the following week.

A bivocational pastor will enjoy balance in regard to work when he can perform his work duties to the best of his ability while still scheduling time for God, family, church, and self.

Family

We have all heard the horror stories of how pastors have neglected their families while ministering to the needs of a church. Many well-known Christian leaders and pastors have looked back over their lives and wished they had spent more time with their families. Billy Graham, commenting about how grateful he is for his life, also admitted, "I have many regrets. . . . For one thing, I would speak less and study more, and I would spend more time with my family."[1]

A pastor once told me that his wife was close to having a nervous breakdown before he even knew she was experiencing any problems. He admitted he was not close to his adult children because he had placed ministry demands ahead of the needs of his family. The real shocker is that he later criticized me because I admitted I could attend one of my daughter's basketball games and not be concerned about ministry work I could be doing. This pastor, like many others, was so committed to the ministry God had given him that he forgot the ministry to his family, which was also God given.

Too often, pastors excuse their neglect of their families, believing it is part of the cost of doing ministry. How can a wife argue when her pastor husband explains that he cannot spend an evening with her because he must be about the work of God?

Bill Hybels, pastor of Willow Creek Community Church, took that approach with his wife, Lynne. While becoming one of the most recognized pastors in America today, Hybels nearly destroyed his marriage. The Hybels are refreshingly candid as they describe how the demands of ministry affected their marriage and the actions that were required to save it. When his wife would ask him to stay home an evening with her, he would respond with, "Kids are dying and going to hell, and you want me to stay home and hold your hand?" He later realized that, while he loved his wife, he was satisfied with a mediocre marriage. His commitment was to the church. "I was busy building a church. I was busy developing a staff. I was busy leading people to Christ." When he finally realized the pain he had caused his wife, he committed himself to rebuild his marriage, but it was almost too late. "[My wife] had been so wounded by my neglect that she responded to my dramatic turnaround with little more than indifference for nearly two years."[2]

When a second job is added to the demands of ministry, a bivocational pastor has even less time for his family, unless he makes the time. Remember, you get done what you spend time doing. If you want to enjoy a healthy family life, you must set that as a priority in your life and make time to work at it.

A few years ago, my wife and I decided our time together was so limited that we had to set aside some time just for ourselves. We started dating every Friday night. We usually go into a nearby city, have a nice dinner, and do some shopping. My wife enjoys collecting Boyd's Bears, and we can usually find one she does not yet have. I enjoy reading, so we often spend some time in one of the larger bookstores in the city. Regardless of what we do, we are together. We can talk and laugh and not have to worry about the telephone interrupting us. Believe me, we protect our Friday night date time zealously! The church not only understands how important this time is to us, they are pleased that we care enough about our thirty-three-year marriage to set aside this time to date.

Both of our children were active in sports during their school days. Our daughter played basketball in junior high school and ran track in high school. Our son also played basketball in junior high school and played baseball in high school. I can count on one hand the number of times I missed one of their games. My wife and I were often the only parents who attended some of the track meets held at other schools, but we wanted our children to know that we cared about what they were doing. Our children are now grown, married, and living in other states. The times we spent together at their activities are some of the special memories we have as a family that can never be taken from us.

Keeping balance in a family, however, involves more than making time for family activities. It also involves maintaining a realistic set of expectations. Some pastors' children are expected to set the example of how children are supposed to behave. But children have enough pressures growing up in today's world. They should not have to be living illustrations for sermons as well. It is a mistake to expect more from pastors' children than from other children in the church.

One summer our son had an opportunity to play Amateur Athletic Union (AAU) basketball for an excellent coach. However, our son came to his mother and me with a problem. Some of the games would take place on Sunday, and the coach was going to call me to ask if our son could miss church on those days. Knowing how important I believe church attendance is, our son was not sure how I would respond. Although the schedule was not yet complete, the coach assured me that there would be few games scheduled on Sunday. My wife and I discussed the situation and agreed that our son could miss church on those Sundays when he had a game.

Our son understood we were not saying that playing basketball was more important than attending a church service, and I do not remember him asking if he could miss a church service to attend any other function. As it turned out, he missed only three or four Sunday morning services that summer, and he usually made it back in time for the evening service on those Sundays. He had a positive AAU experience, and he learned a little about living a balanced Christian life.

Please do not mistakenly believe that we are the perfect Christian family or that I have never made a mistake with my family.

Marriage and family life are always growing experiences, and much growth comes through mistakes that are made. One thing I do know, however, is that pastors come and go. My wife has only one husband, and our children have only one father. God has given every husband and father certain responsibilities, and I have never read in the Bible that being a pastor negated those responsibilities. If I pastored the largest church in America and lost my family, I would be a failure as a husband, a father, and a pastor. We cannot neglect our famlies and believe we are doing God's will as ministers. We must give our families high priority.

Church

Every pastor wants to be an effective leader in the church he serves. He wants to see people's lives changed as a result of his ministry, and he wants to see the church develop and become all that God wants it to be. Unfortunately, these desires can sometimes lead a pastor to believe he must make these things happen at any cost. This section is difficult to write because of recent events in our region, but the events I'm about to describe show the importance of this topic.

One of the larger churches in our region suffered a fire that caused serious damage to its facility. The following day, the pastor committed suicide. He left a note in which he admitted to setting the fire because the church had been resisting making a decision he believed they needed to make. He thought the fire would push them toward that decision. Evidently, following the fire, he realized what he had done and could not live with his actions.

This pastor was not some wild-eyed lunatic who ministered on the fringe. He was a highly respected pastor who had tremendous leadership in his church and denomination. He led a revival at a nearby church, and I heard it had been a positive experience. He led deacon retreats for churches and served in various positions at the state level.

I do not pretend to know what went through his mind, nor do I know if anyone knows for sure what he was thinking. My sense is that he felt, like many pastors, that he was responsible for making things happen in the church. When things did not happen the way he thought they needed to, he may have felt the result was due to a failure of his leadership.

As pastors, we must remind ourselves that we are not the head of the church. Jesus Christ is the head of the church, and we are called by him to lead his church. Too often, we feel that we must push the church in certain directions. Such an attitude will often lead to problems in our ministry and in our church. Pastors are called to lead their congregations, not to push them. Congregations must decide if they will follow in the direction they are being led. If not, the church and the leader need to find a common vision.

A bivocational pastor may certainly run into this problem in the church he serves. Tradition often plays a major role in small churches, which are most apt to call a bivocational pastor. Change will not come easily, if at all. And if it does come, it will take time. Trust must be developed between the church and the pastor or there will be no change. As we all know, trust takes time to develop, but it can be destroyed very quickly. If a congregation begins to feel that their pastor is trying to push them, they will resist not only the change that is being forced on them but also the leadership of the pastor.

Balance in ministry requires that a pastor understand he is not responsible for making things happen in a church. He is called to serve, to lead, to pray, and to trust God. Perhaps a church decides not to go in a certain direction because the members have a better understanding of God's vision than the pastor has. Pastors sometimes think they are the only ones who can hear from God, but that is not so. It could be that the pastor has missed God's direction in this particular situation, or it may be that he has misunderstood God's timing for a change to occur. Members may not be responding as he hoped because God has not yet moved in their hearts to make the change.

There may be many reasons why a church does not follow the leading of a pastor, and these reasons do not necessarily indicate a failure on the part of the pastor. It also does not mean that the pastor is authorized by God to do everything possible to make something happen in the church. Balance in ministry means that a pastor leads according to what he believes is God's will and then leaves the results up to God.

The pastor who took his life left behind a wife and small children who loved him, a church who needed him, a community who respected him, and friends who admired him. All have been deeply hurt and confused by his actions, which were based on an unbalanced view of ministry that led him to accept more responsibility than God gives to any pastor.

It is also difficult for a pastor to maintain a level of balance because he ends each day with unfinished business. In my work in the factory, we built a certain number of engines on the assembly line each day. We knew when our work was done.

Pastoral work is not like that. When a pastor ends his work for the day, he always knows there was one more visit he could have—and perhaps should have—made. Additional phone calls could have been made. More preparation for the next committee meeting could have been done. Perhaps he has not yet started preparing his sermon for the next Sunday. People within the shadow of the church are still lost.

Some pastors who struggle with this do so because they have never learned how to delegate. Small churches often look at their pastor as the one responsible for all the work of ministry in their church. Unfortunately, some pastors see themselves in the same light.

While attending a state convention one year, I talked to an area minister about my frustration with how things were going at my church. He politely listened and then told me I was doing all the work in the church, and that by doing so, I was depriving members of the opportunity to grow as individuals. I needed to allow those who had accepted positions of ministry to fulfill their responsibilities.

The next Sunday I apologized to the congregation during my sermon. That certainly got everyone's attention! I went on to tell them how I was depriving them of opportunities to grow by doing all the work they did not do. I announced that from that time on anyone who accepted a responsibility in the church would be expected to fulfill that responsibility. I would provide whatever resources and assistance were needed, but I would no longer do their work for them. If someone accepted a responsibility and did not fulfill it, the job would be left undone. If asked about it, I would refer the questioner to whoever had accepted the responsibility. Our church responded well, and we have grown as a result of more people fulfilling their responsibilities.

Pastors need to heed the advice that Moses' father-in-law, Jethro, gave him in Exodus 18. He saw how Moses was trying to minister to the needs of the people by himself. In verse 18 he told Moses, "Both you and these people who are with you will surely wear yourselves out. For this thing is too much for you; you are not able to perform it by yourself." He advised Moses to train others to do part of the work.

God has called every believer to a place of ministry in his church, and the Holy Spirit has equipped each one with the gifts necessary to fulfill that ministry. Pastors need to allow members to fulfill their calling and stop believing that pastors alone are responsible for doing all the work that needs to be done in the church. Everyone will benefit from this change in attitude.

God

One of the ironies I have found in ministry is that the demands of ministry can lead a pastor to ignore his relationship with God. I first noticed it while attending Bible school. I spent a great deal of time studying the Bible and books about the Bible for my class assignments. I also spent time studying while preparing sermons. But one day I realized that I was not spending any time developing my relationship with God. I was learning a lot *about* God, but I was not spending any time *with* God.

I have talked to a number of seminary students who have told me that they experienced the same problem. However, the problem does not end with seminary. Pastors often continue to struggle with balancing their devotional lives with the demands of ministry, which are great and often require much time. When we do find the time to study the Bible, we do so to prepare sermons. Our prayers are often on behalf of some individual who has expressed a need for prayer. Our own spiritual development is too often hurt by the ministry work we do.

God calls us to *be* something before he calls us to *do* something. He calls us to spend time with him so we can grow into spiritual maturity. Out of that growth will come much more effective ministry. W. A. Criswell wrote that "the ultimate and abiding secret strength of the pastor lies in his daily walk with God."[3] H. B. London and Neil B. Wiseman agree: Personal spiritual growth is absolutely essential for a pastor if he wants to enjoy sustained satisfactions and beneficial ministry.[4]

Every year at my second job, we took an inventory of every item in our factory. Most churches file an annual report with their denomination that measures their ministry effectiveness. We need to do the same on a personal level by taking a periodic inventory of our lives at least once a year if not more often. One of the areas of examination should be our personal spiritual development. Do I have a regular time of devotional reading and prayer? Have I grown closer to God since the last inventory? Growth in such areas as love and faith may be difficult to measure, but we must try. If growth has occurred, we need to continue that growth. If it appears our spiritual growth has suffered since the last inventory, we need to take steps to improve it.

Churches need to understand that a pastor's personal spiritual growth is important to them as well as to the pastor. He may need to spend a day every few months alone with God. Some pastors check into a hotel for a day with just their Bible, while others visit a retreat facility for a time of quiet reflection. Churches need to provide their pastors with a book allowance that enables them to purchase devotional books to help in their spiritual development. Vacations and time away from the church should be generously given so a pastor can refresh his spirit and his walk with God.

My wife and I often choose to go to the ocean for vacation. Nothing brings me closer to God than to sit on the balcony of our hotel early in the morning while watching and listening to the waves crash onto the shore. I try to be up before the sun rises above the horizon to catch those first rays of light as they hit the water's surface. I have never failed to marvel at God's creation at such times and to be in awe that I am a part of that creation.

A pastor's ability to effectively minister is in direct proportion to his personal spiritual development. Any pastor can minister on his own power for a time, but burnout will eventually set in if he does not maintain his relationship with the true source of his power.

Let me help you with your inventory. How are you doing spiritually? What are you doing to continue your spiritual development? If improvement is needed in this area, can you think of any good reason why you cannot start today?

Self

If we are going to spend several hours a week at a second job, several hours in ministry, and time with God and our families, when will we have time to spend on ourselves? Many pastors are never able to find the answer to this question, and they suffer greatly as a result. I know because I was one of them.

In December of 1987 I graduated from Boyce Bible School. Four very difficult years of study were behind me, and I was excited about the future. Within a few months, however, I began experiencing some problems. I was depressed. I was physically, emotionally, and spiritually exhausted. Every Sunday it was a struggle to walk to the pulpit to begin my sermon. All I wanted to do was run out the back door and keep on running. Fortunately, I never did.

The depression grew worse until one day I started crying uncontrollably in our dining room. My wife walked to the telephone, called our physician, and made an appointment for that afternoon. My doctor diagnosed me with clinical depression and prescribed medication. I asked his opinion about counseling, and he encouraged me to pursue it if I felt it would be helpful. I contacted a Christian counseling service and made an appointment for the following week. The counselor agreed with my doctor that I was depressed, and we began weekly counseling sessions. For almost a year I remained on the medication and met with my counselor. In many ways, I lost a year of my life, but I also learned some important things about myself. I also learned that I have to take time out for myself and I need to take care of myself.

Before my bout with depression, it was not uncommon for me to go for days on two or three hours of sleep each night. Meals were often eaten in the car while on my way to the next event in my life. I was overweight, and a lack of exercise and poor nutrition had made that problem even worse. I also had decided to bypass the typical midlife transition in favor of a full-blown midlife crisis at the same time all these other events were occurring in my life.[5] It is no wonder I became depressed.

To make matters even worse, no one knew about my problems except my wife and children. The church never knew I had any problems until a couple of years after I was again healthy. I had the mistaken belief that the sheep would not want a sick shepherd. A few members knew I was having problems, but none of them had any idea how serious it was until I shared my story in a sermon about two years after my recovery.

A lack of balance caused me to become ill and to lose an entire year of enjoyable living. I was trying to meet everyone's needs except my own. I learned the hard way that exercise, proper nutrition, rest, and times of relaxation are all necessary if I want to remain healthy. I've tried to put what I learned into practice.

My wife and I enjoy fishing, so a few years ago I purchased a boat so we can enjoy an occasional day of fishing. Last year when I was preparing to take early retirement from my factory job, our children bought me a set of golf clubs as a combination

Father's Day and retirement gift. Fishing or playing a round of golf helps me relax and stay mentally alert. While working at my desk I may take a ten-minute break and play a game on my computer. That mini-break is relaxing and lets me concentrate better when I return to work. During the first several years of my pastorate, I never took both weeks of vacation the church gave me. I now get four weeks of vacation, and you better believe I take them! And I am a better pastor because of it.

Several months ago I joined a health club, and I try to be there most mornings when it opens. I spend thirty minutes on a treadmill and follow that with some light exercises. I have seen a definite improvement in my stamina and energy levels since beginning my program.

Diet and sleep are two other components of a healthy lifestyle that I try to watch. When I keep these elements of my life in proper balance, I feel better and I work better. The problems I encounter in ministry generate less stress, which means I can minister to others better.

Taking time out for ourselves is not selfish or poor stewardship of our time. It also does not mean we are neglecting our ministry. I used to tell people that I would rather burn out than rust out. Now I know that is not a right way to think. Either way I am out.

ALLOW FOR MARGIN

If there is one book I wish I had read at the beginning of my ministry it is *Margin* by Richard A. Swenson. Although the book was not written specifically for pastors, every pastor should make a point to read it and put its ideas into practice. Dr. Swenson defines margin as "the gap between rest and exhaustion, the space between breathing freely and suffocating."[6] He goes on to say that "to be healthy, we require margin in at least four areas: emotional energy, physical energy, time, and finances."[7]

My depression came when I had no margin in my life. I had all the plates spinning and all the balls in the air, but there was no room for anything else. My life was filled to the brim. The first unexpected demand on my time sent me crashing into depression as my body's systems shut down.

How many pastors have you heard brag about how full their calendars are? They appear to equate busyness with spirituality. To such pastors I share a question from Swenson's book: "Is God now proexhaustion? Doesn't he lead people beside the still waters anymore?"[8] Unfortunately, too many of us pastors want to preach encouraging words to our congregation about slowing down and reducing the stress in their lives while we model the exact opposite in our own lives.

Build margin into your life. Take your day planner and schedule some time each week for pleasure reading, for a relaxing hobby, for time spent with your family, or for time just spent under a shade tree. When someone calls to ask you to do something, you can honestly refuse because you have a previous appointment at that time. You will feel better, be more productive, and be better equipped to handle emergencies when they do occur.

ONLY YOU CAN ENSURE BALANCE IN YOUR LIFE

As a bivocational pastor, you will have to set priorities for the use of your time. No one else should be allowed to control your schedule. There is no way you will be able to satisfy the expectations that every person in your life will have for you. Pastors often find it difficult to say no to any request, but if you do not develop the ability to refuse some requests, your life will soon be out of balance and you will be miserable.

It is important to educate the members of your church early in your ministry so they understand the priorities you have established. Those priorities need to be emphasized occasionally to remind others how you are maintaining balance in your life. If your priorities do not match those that the congregation believes are proper, you may need to discuss them with the leadership of your church. If compromise cannot be achieved or if the church refuses to honor your priorities, it may be an indication that this church is not the right place of service for you.

The priorities I have established for my life and ministry are: (1) God, (2) family, (3) church, (4) work, and (5) self. I do not claim that these are the right priorities for everyone. Each person must set his own priorities in order to achieve the necessary balance in life and ministry. Nor do I pretend that these priorities are etched in stone and must be strictly followed at all times. As J. Grant Howard reminds us, "At times we have to emphasize certain relationships and certain responsibilities . . . because of *present needs.*"[9]

There may be days when the demands of the church will mean that it will take priority over the needs of family. However, those times should be measured in hours, or, at most, in days. For example, our church just completed a week of Vacation Bible School. Every evening demanded our involvement at the church. Even my Friday night date with my wife was postponed because we had the commencement program on that night, but this is the exception and not the rule.

You get done what you spend time doing. If you want a balanced life and a balanced ministry, it will happen only if you make it happen. I suffered a painful year of depression because I did not maintain balance in my life when I began my ministry. I hope you will learn from my mistake.

Balance also requires that you maintain healthy expectations for your ministry, church, and family. Demanding too much of yourself can lead to burnout and possible personal tragedy. Attempting to force your church to make decisions they do not want to make will only stiffen their resistance and probably shorten your tenure as pastor. Besides, God has called us to lead our churches, not push them. Too many pastors' wives and children have grown bitter and abandoned the Christian faith because of unrealistic expectations placed on them. For their sake, and yours, do not ignore their needs and do not try to force them into a mold of your expectations.

In order to be an effective and healthy bivocational pastor, you need to balance the various demands on your time, and you need to maintain healthy expectations for yourself and others. When you find balance in these areas of your life, you will experience the joy of bivocational ministry.

SEVEN

THE IMPORTANCE
OF PREACHING

Much of a bivocational pastor's public ministry will take place in the pulpit. In a large church, the pastor may provide leadership through the pastoral staff or through various committees or boards. In a small church, there are fewer committees for the pastor to lead, and he is often the only staff member. He will probably not receive many requests for formal counseling. Visiting the members and prospective members of the church will be an important part of a bivocational pastor's ministry, but his pulpit ministry will be the one that will provide him with the greatest opportunity to teach and lead his congregation. A bivocational pastor, therefore, needs to understand that his preaching ministry must receive his best effort.

Bivocational pastors usually realize this but feel at a disadvantage because of a lack of formal training in sermon preparation. Many feel they have inadequate skills for planning, preparing, and delivering quality sermons week after week. Some rely entirely on divine inspiration, but most of us know that the harder we work and study the more inspired we become. The sermon that just flows through our mind is welcome but often rare. As we prepare two or three sermons each week, we know that many hours are likely to be spent planning a topic, studying commentaries, and formulating our thoughts so we can present a sermon that our congregation will understand and find helpful. Without formal training, sermon preparation can seem an impossible task, but it does not have to be. This chapter will suggest several things a bivocational pastor can do to improve his pulpit ministry.

TALK WITH OTHER MINISTERS

Bivocational ministers often find it difficult to be part of a formal ministerial association because of work schedules. That is unfortunate because a great way to get ideas for sermons is by talking with other pastors about their messages.

One of the joys I had working in the factory was that there were a number of bivocational ministers who also worked there. In fact, for several years many of us worked on the same assembly line together. We took our breaks and lunches together. Often our talk centered around sermon ideas we had or recent messages we had delivered. When one of us would share a particular thought, someone in our group would usually say, "Wait a minute while I get a pencil and some paper." It became one of our standing jokes, but the fact is we all got seeds for sermons from our times of sharing. Those were some of the richest fellowship times I have ever known in my life.

No one would call our group a ministerial association, but it functioned as one. We were able to pray for one another, study Scripture together, and grow in our relationship with God. We were from various church backgrounds and denominations, but we often visited each other's churches when something special was taking place, and we even occasionally preached at revivals or filled pulpits for one another. But some of the most special times were when we shared with one another what God was showing us in our studies. I believe our sharing enriched our preaching.

Perhaps there are other bivocational ministers in your place of employment with whom you could share, or perhaps other ministers in your community cannot attend regular ministerial group meetings. Just because a ministerial group exists in your community does not mean there may not be a need for another one. Many years ago a second women's mission group was started in our church because many of the younger women were working outside the home and could not meet during the day. Within a few years, the new group was larger than the original group. Talk to some of the other ministers in your area, especially those of small churches, and see if they have a need to spend time with other ministers. Start your own group of ministers who can pray for one another and support one another. Talking with other pastors and sharing sermon ideas can help you in preparation and study.

FIND A MENTOR

Any minister would profit from a good mentor relationship. Unfortunately, a bivocational pastor may discover it is difficult to find a good mentor. The problem frequently has to do with a lack of time. Because of work schedules and other demands, it is often difficult to find the time to develop a mentor relationship with another minister. That does not mean a bivocational minister cannot learn from and be influenced by other ministers.

To be honest, the ministers who have mentored me are some of my favorite authors. My preaching ministry has been greatly influenced by Charles Swindoll, John MacArthur Jr., Billy Graham, Robert Schuller, Charles Colson, and James Dobson. Even though I have never had the privilege of meeting any of these men and developing a relationship with them, I consider them to be my mentors in the ministry.

Although I do not have every book Charles Swindoll has written, I have most of them. Whenever possible I listen to his radio program. He has taught me how to go beyond the clichés that dominate so much of preaching today and speak the truths of God's Word in ways that are fresh and interesting. While never deviating from the integrity of Scripture, he challenges his audiences with the truths of the Bible in ways that contemporary people can understand and to which they can respond.

He has also taught me that the life of the pastor, and every Christian, should be one of joy. Anyone who has heard his radio broadcast has enjoyed his infectious laughter from the pulpit. Here is a pastor who has fun while preaching and ministering! For some ministers that may be a revolutionary idea, but our congregations and the unchurched in our communities need to know that Christianity should produce genuine joy in the lives of believers. Swindoll commented in one book that he received a letter from a woman who wrote how much his teachings meant to her. Her only request was that he never take the laughter out of his broadcasts because "yours is the only laughter that comes into our home."[1] As pastors, we each need to bring laughter into the lives of those we serve. Swindoll has given me permission to do that.

John MacArthur Jr. keeps reminding me of the value of expository preaching. Such preaching allows God to speak to our congregations, promotes biblical literacy among our members, and transforms both the preacher and the congregation.[2] Although I occasionally do preach topical messages on timely issues, most of my sermons are expository because I believe that they provide the most long-term benefit to our congregation.

I have mentioned elsewhere that each year I preach through a book of the Bible or a major section of Scripture. Such preaching ensures that I neither simply preach on my favorite topics nor just recycle my sermons every three or four years. Expository preaching allows more time to be spent on sermon preparation because I am spending less time trying to decide on a topic.

MacArthur has written a number of commentaries that I have found helpful in my preparation of expository sermons. His long tenure as pastor of Grace Community Church and his faithfulness to expository preaching have inspired me as a bivocational pastor.

Billy Graham has also been an inspiration to thousands of pastors for a number of decades. Two things about his ministry have influenced my own. One is his simple presentation of the gospel. Like the apostle Paul, Billy Graham has never tried to impress his listeners with clever oratory. He has simply lifted up Christ so all would be drawn to him. Multitudes have come to a saving relationship with Jesus Christ because of Graham's faithfulness to the ministry God has given him.

The second area of Billy Graham's life and ministry that has influenced mine is his integrity. Year after year he is recognized as the most respected person in American religion. When so many ministers have been touched by financial and moral scandals, neither have ever touched Billy Graham or his ministry. Multitudes of people have responded to his sermons because they trust him and his message.

Very early in Graham's ministry he made two decisions that would help him avoid even the appearance of evil. He would never be alone with a woman who was not his wife, and he would never handle any of the money his ministry generated. It is easy to see the wisdom of those decisions, and I have emulated them in my own ministry.

It is not enough to study and prepare sermons. The messenger must be trusted before his listeners will trust his message. Throughout this book we have seen that trust is essential to pastoral leadership. Trust is also necessary for a successful pulpit ministry. Billy Graham's integrity over several decades of ministry should be an example to every minister.

Another mentor of mine is Robert Schuller. Often controversial, Schuller was successfully reaching out to the unchurched long before "seekers" and "user-friendly churches" became the buzzwords they are today. Before Bill Hybels and Rick Warren, Robert Schuller was speaking to the unchurched in his community in terms they understood. These people were willing to come to worship services each week because Schuller understood their concerns and attempted to answer their questions about faith and

God. He has taught me the value of understanding the unchurched in our community.

Schuller has also taught me the importance of the positive sermon. In his books and speaking, Schuller is always positive. He wants to lift up his reading and listening audiences. He seeks to inspire, not beat people into submission.

About two years ago I became convicted that too many of my sermons were negative and harsh. People often spend six days being beaten down by life, by work, and by other people. Why would they want to come to church if they know the preacher is also going to beat on them? Why would members invite their unchurched friends to attend church if the message is going to be critical and negative? Please understand, every sermon was not like that, but some were.

After studying Schuller, Hybels, Warren, and others, I made the decision that I would not preach any more negative sermons. I would still call sin what it was, and the gospel would not be compromised. I would not be afraid to say, "Thus saith the Lord." But my sermons would be presented in a positive way that would inspire as well as challenge. It is just as easy to say, "These are the things we need to do" as it is to say, "These are the things you must not do."

I announced this decision to the church by confessing that I believed some of my sermons were too harsh. Jesus had called the weary to him so they might be refreshed, not so he could wear them down even more. I told the church of my intention to preach sermons that would be positive and helpful. They would never need to be afraid to invite their unchurched friends to attend services with them.

This proved to be a good decision. I receive many comments from members of our church about the helpfulness of my messages. A few people have taken copies of sermons to other people so they could read a particular message. The church has grown numerically as people have invited others to attend church, and several people have commented about the exciting spirit that prevails in our church services.

The final two men I listed were Charles Colson and James Dobson. While neither man is a pastor or preacher, both have had a great influence on my ministry. They have challenged me to see social, political, and family issues as moral issues that need to be addressed from a biblical perspective. Pastors must be at the forefront of speaking about such issues as abortion, euthanasia, justice, civil rights, and violence. Not only do these men challenge me, and countless other pastors, to speak on these and other issues, they also educate us about these issues. Both are excellent writers, and both often speak about the problems of our culture and the spiritual answers that are needed. They have given me the knowledge I need to inform my congregation about these issues.

Another thing that impresses me about these men is the energy they put into their work. Such energy is given only when a person feels a genuine passion about his or her work. I admire people who have a passion for what they do, and it is obvious to me that Colson and Dobson are passionate about their ministries. I always want to have that same passion.

These six men are my mentors, and they have influenced my ministry in many ways. As valuable as they have been to my ministry, however, I must make sure I never make the mistake of copying them in an effort to become a better minister. God has not called me to be an imitation of Charles Swindoll or Billy Graham. He has called me to use the gifts and the personality I have to serve him in a particular place at a particular time.

God has also called you, not your imitation of another preacher. Find mentors who can help you develop into a better minister, but never think that you need to become a carbon copy of anyone else. If God had wanted that other person in your place of service, he would have put him there. Instead, he brought you to that place, and you need to serve him to the best of your ability.

SET ASIDE TIME TO STUDY

Every week you will be expected to preach to your congregation. Depending on the number of services your church has, you may need to prepare a hundred or more sermons during the course of a year. Sermon preparation is going to require a significant amount of your time each week.

My favorite professor at Boyce Bible School did not give tests. He required his students to write various papers throughout the semester that demonstrated how much we were learning about the material we were studying. This professor also had a very simple rule about the papers: If they were late, for any reason, the student received a zero for that paper. No paper would be accepted after the day on which it was due.

As good students are supposed to do, we moaned and complained about such a strict rule. We offered several perfectly good reasons why a paper might be late, but none of our reasons changed his mind. He explained that because we were ministerial students we needed to understand the importance of working with deadlines, and we needed to understand that people would expect us to fulfill our ministerial duties regardless of what might be happening in our lives. As pastors we would be expected to preach a sermon every Sunday. We would not be able to step up to the pulpit, shrug our shoulders, and say, "Sorry, folks, but I just didn't have time to put anything together this week." Of course, he was right.

Pastors need to inform their congregations of the importance of their study time. Many laypeople have no idea how long it takes to prepare a sermon because no one has ever told them. Encourage some of your lay leaders to preach while you are away on vacation. After doing so, they will probably better appreciate the amount of time you spend preparing sermons each week. When the members of your church better understand how much time is required for sermon preparation, they will be less likely to interrupt that time with trivial matters.

We must set aside sufficient time each week to prepare ourselves to teach God's Word to his people. W. A. Criswell encourages pastors to set aside their mornings for prayer, study, and sermon preparation.[3] Once again, a bivocational pastor finds himself at a disadvantage because of other commitments. Most bivocational pastors would love to follow that advice, but their mornings may already be given to their second job. However, with some planning, it is possible to find sufficient time to adequately prepare the sermons you will preach each week.

SET ASIDE A PLACE TO STUDY

It is much easier to study when a specific place has been set aside for that study. A pastor needs a place where his resources are easily available, a place that is quiet, and a place that is comfortable. Such a place may not always be at the church. Because a bivocational pastor's study time will often come in small bits of time, it may make more sense to have his office in his house.

For several years I kept my library in my office at the church. Much of my studying is done at night, and it seldom made sense for me to drive the seven miles from our house to the church to study. In all honesty, a lot of my sermons have been prepared after I have pulled off my shoes, put on my pajamas, and fixed myself a late-night snack! Too often, however, I found that a book or commentary I needed for my study was at the church. If I was studying at the church, of course, the material I needed was at the house. Either way, my study was disrupted.

The problem was finally resolved when I moved my study to one room of our house. All of my books and other study helps are in that room. When I am finished studying for the evening, I can leave my materials, notes, and everything else on my desk until the next time. My study time is now much more efficient.

PREACH A SERIES OF SERMONS

Some ministers spend too much time trying to decide what they are going to preach on, which reduces the amount of time they have to actually prepare the sermon. The best way around this problem is by preaching series of sermons. If I am preaching through a book of the Bible, I never wonder what I am going to preach about the next Sunday. The text tells me. This allows me more time to study the passage so I can share its meaning with the congregation.

Preaching series of sermons also helps a minister in his planning. Most preaching textbooks recommend that a pastor plan his preaching several weeks in advance. Some pastors are able to plan their next quarter's preaching schedule; some even plan their schedules a year in advance. This is a difficult task for a minister who primarily preaches topical sermons. When preaching a series of sermons, such planning is much easier, and this planning helps a minister make the best use of his study time.

MAKE GOOD USE OF RESOURCES

Good commentaries are essential tools in sermon preparation, and good tools can help a bivocational pastor overcome some of his time limitations. However, not all commentaries are created equal. Some are written from a liberal perspective. Some require a much greater knowledge of the Hebrew and Greek languages than many bivocational pastors have. Others simply do not go deep enough into the text to be of any value to a minister. Ministers should take the time to study commentaries before investing money in something that may be of little help.

A number of companies now have Bible study programs for computers. Many of these programs include several translations of the Bible as well as maps, outlines, Hebrew and Greek word studies, and Bible dictionaries and commentaries. Several companies offer their customers different levels of programs, ranging from basic programs with few resources to more advanced programs with dozens of study helps. A minister can choose which program he wants to buy based on his needs and the amount of money he is willing to spend. These programs often contain dozens of additional resources that can be added to a system. A simple phone call to the manufacturer is all it takes to purchase these other resources.

A minister with Internet access can find hundreds of web sites dedicated to Bible study and sermon preparation. These web sites vary greatly in quality, so it is important to review them before you might need them. However, this is a resource that should not be overlooked.

Commentaries and other Bible study helps can be expensive, but there are ways to reduce that expense. Used bookstores sometimes carry theological books at very low prices. You can also find bookstores that specialize in used theological books near seminaries, but the prices there may be somewhat higher than in other used bookstores. Some community libraries have used book sales to raise money for the library. Not only do they sell old library books, but individuals often donate books to be sold. I attend the one at our library every year and always bring home at least one sack of books. Last year at the sale I was able to purchase both volumes of the *Theological Wordbook of the Old Testament* by R. Laird Harris, Gleason L. Archer Jr., and Bruce K. Waltke for $1.00. That set normally sells for $69.99.

Unfortunately, such bargains are seldom found. Books are expensive, and their cost should not be borne entirely by a pastor. A church needs to understand that books and other resources are tools that their pastor must have in order to better serve them. A church's budget should include provisions for this expense.[4]

Our church's budget groups books, periodicals, and other resources under "reimbursement for ministry-related expenses." Each year a dollar amount is established for this category, and I am reimbursed up to that amount for any book or other resource I purchase. I pay for any additional materials that exceed the set limit. As a reimbursable expense, I do not have to pay income tax on this amount. Such a plan is fair to the church and to the minister.

STRIVE FOR EXCELLENCE IN PREACHING

Throughout this book, we have seen the positive results that occur when a pastor can remain at a church for a long period of time. However, a longer pastorate forces a bivocational pastor to continually improve his pulpit ministry. We said earlier that a pastor may have to preach one hundred or more sermons a year. Multiply that by a ten-year pastorate, and a pastor has one thousand sermons to prepare and deliver. He will also find himself preaching to many of the same people each week who have come to hear a fresh word from God.

With proper sermon planning and preparation, a pastor can deliver a fresh message to those people. Swindoll encourages those of us who preach when he writes:

> In this day of shallow sermonettes, syrupy devotionals, and highly emotional tirades that lack scriptural substance, if you prepare and deliver interesting messages that are sourced in Scripture, you will become the talk of the community. More importantly, your flock will become better equipped to assist and serve effectively in the work of the ministry.[5]

One benefit of a longer pastorate is that it gives a minister time to improve his preaching skills. I have learned that when the members of the church know their pastor loves them, they can be very forgiving of poor sermons. More than once I have felt that my sermon on a particular Sunday was poor, but I have never in eighteen years been criticized for a poor sermon.

A bivocational pastor I know was approached by one of his deacons who told him that the quality of his sermons had improved over the years. The deacon told the pastor that his sermons were of average quality when he began his ministry in the church, but he had seen a marked improvement over the past several months. The pastor greatly appreciated the compliment because this deacon was one who had always spoken honestly and from the heart. The pastor had been trying to improve the quality of his sermons over the years, and this deacon's comments made him feel his hard work had been worthwhile.

Another pastor friend recently told me that one of his deacons was ready to tune him out one Sunday after he read the Scripture text. The deacon was certain he knew what the message would be because he had heard many sermons preached on that text. However, the pastor's opening statements got his attention, and the deacon soon realized the pastor was approaching that passage of Scripture from a new perspective. He later told the pastor how much he enjoyed the sermon. The pastor was greatly encouraged by the comments because he had also been working hard to improve his preaching.

Preaching is hard work, but it is also rewarding work. It takes a great deal of commitment to develop and present sermons each week, but your people deserve your very best effort in the pulpit. God's Word has the power to change people's lives, and you have the opportunity to teach that Word. When you see their lives begin to change because of what they have learned, you will know that your hard work has been well worth the effort.

EIGHT

BIVOCATIONAL MINISTRY
MAY BE FOR YOU

South Park Baptist Church in Oklahoma, a church with 550 members, is currently involved in a major building program. That does not sound unusual, until you learn that the pastor is bivocational. Leon Wilson served as a fully funded pastor for twenty years and then made the decision to become bivocational. He has been a bivocational pastor for twenty-five years and also serves as a bivocational consultant for the Southern Baptist Convention. In addition to Pastor Wilson, the church has four more ministers on staff, all of whom are bivocational by choice.

Jimmy Reader was also a fully funded pastor for twenty years before choosing to become bivocational to help his church when it encountered some problems. This American Baptist pastor also serves on the Senate of the denomination's Minister's Council. With his encouragement, the Minister's Council recently took steps to create a network of bivocational ministers in the denomination. This pastor loves his church and believes in the importance of bivocational ministry. He recently wrote a booklet entitled "Another Look at Bivocational Ministry," which was published by the Minister's Council.

Larry Orange serves as a bivocational director of missions in Kentucky. In this capacity, he serves twenty-six churches, all but one of which are led by bivocational pastors. In 1996, Orange had the privilege of conducting a recognition service for four of his association's bivocational pastors who had a combined total of 182 years of service.[1] His commitment to this type of ministry can be seen in the fact that he is currently teaching a class on bivocational ministry at Boyce Bible School.

Here are three individuals who serve in bivocational ministries because they believe in this type of ministry, and their work has been successful and rewarding. These men are living examples of what I believe God is going to do in the hearts and lives of many he will call into ministry.

We have spent several chapters studying bivocational ministry. Perhaps some of you have thought about going into such a ministry. You may be among those whom God called into ministry later in life and who do not feel called to leave their jobs to begin a full-time ministry in a church. Perhaps it is a bivocational ministry that you feel specifically called to enter. How can you know if God has called you to serve as a bivocational pastor? This chapter contains a number of questions that may help you make this determination. Although I will suggest some possible answers, the only answers that really count are your answers.

HAVE YOU BEEN CALLED TO THE MINISTRY?

The most important thing for any pastor is that he has been called by God into a position of ministry. Like Paul, we must say, "I became a minister according to the gift of the grace of God given to me by the effective working of His power" (Eph. 3:7). Nothing is more essential for a successful ministry than to be certain of one's call into the ministry. At times, the certainty of the call will be the only thing that will sustain a minister during difficult times. This is true for bivocational ministers as well as for those who are fully supported by their churches. Few things are more damaging to a church or to one's own faith than for someone to attempt to minister without having been called by God to the task.

Unfortunately, there is not an easy way to determine if God has called you to a place of service. Few of us will have an experience such as Moses had at the burning bush or Isaiah had when he saw the Lord high and lifted up. Most of us will simply have an "inescapable conviction that God has his hand upon us."[2] There will be an awareness that God has given the spiritual gifts and the natural abilities that will be needed in ministry.[3] We also need to be certain we meet the spiritual qualifications for church leaders that Paul listed in 1 Timothy 3 and Titus 1.

God's call can also come at different times in life and through a variety of ways. W. A. Criswell accepted the call to preach at a revival meeting when he was twelve years old.[4] Charles Swindoll was in the marines planning another career when he began to feel God calling him into the ministry.[5] As a young man, George W. Truett was encouraged by his fellow church members to enter the ministry. Although he first resisted, he eventually yielded to God's call and became one of America's most respected ministers.[6] He would serve as pastor of the First Baptist Church, Dallas, Texas, for forty-seven years.

If we have this sense of calling, it is often wise to discuss it with others. However, God's call is not easily explained to other people. Many in my family wondered about my sanity when I announced that I believed God had called me to be a minister. My wife and I had not been saved for very long, and my life before my salvation had been rather rough. A few of my family members actually became angry when they heard the news. My wife did not know what to think, but, praise God, she supported me.

I could not explain why I believed God had called me to ministry. My pastor agreed with me that God had given me gifts that could be used in pastoral ministry, and our church was willing to give me a license to preach. Some of my Christian co-workers were excited when I shared my sense of God's calling with them, but others with whom I worked thought I had lost my mind. I experienced more opposition than encouragement.

It was eighteen months after my church granted my license to preach before a church invited me to do so. Our director of missions wanted me to begin theological studies before he would give my name to any church that needed someone to supply its pulpit. There were several retired ministers who attended our church, and our pastor would ask them to preach when he was gone. Several times during that eighteen months I wondered if God had truly called me into the ministry.

I was growing discouraged when a church in another denomination asked me to preach at their midweek service. The message that night was less than memorable, but doors of opportunity began to open. I preached in a number of churches until one asked me to serve as their interim pastor. When that ministry ended a few months later, Hebron contacted me about accepting their pastorate.

It would have been easy for me to give up when my ministry opportunities did not look promising. The only reason I did not was that I believed God had called me. God had convinced me even though I was unable to convince others. I was willing to step out in faith to respond to his call as best I could.

IS THERE A NEED?

I heard a preacher once say that the need is the call. He noted that many people claim they would minister in some capacity if they felt called to do so. The point he made was that there are many ministry opportunities around us all the time. We need to respond to those needs, and in doing so we will find the call on our lives.

God needed a man to lead his people out of Egyptian slavery and called Moses. When Moses was nearing the end of his life, God raised up Joshua to complete the task of leading the Israelites into the Promised Land. When the Israelites suffered from a lack of leadership and turned from God, he raised up judges to lead them. God took a young shepherd boy named David and selected him to be the king of Israel. Men such as Isaiah, Jeremiah, Ezekiel, and others would later be called by God to serve as prophets, warning Israel to turn back to God. In every instance, there was a need, and God called individuals to minister to that need. This pattern continues today.

Is there a church in your community that needs a bivocational minister? In our area there are many churches with that need. Many are currently being served by student pastors. A number of them are barely holding on to life. There is little ministry occurring in them because they have not had strong leadership for many years.

Some people believe that God only calls ministers to serve churches that are far from their homes. Quite often, ministers send their profiles to churches in several states. All the time there may be churches nearby that are desperately seeking a pastor who will love and lead them.

Are there churches in your area like this? They will often have fewer than fifty members.[7] The members may be wonderful people and are just in need of pastoral leadership to help them regain the fire their church once had. Perhaps you are the one God wants to provide that leadership. Maybe if you served this church as a bivocational pastor, God would be able to pour out such a blessing that neither the church nor you could hold it all. Sometimes the only thing a church needs to turn around a declining situation is a pastor with a vision and the determination to see that vision fulfilled.[8] I can think of nothing more exciting for a person who has been called by God than to be used to bring a church from the edge of death to new life.

IS YOUR FAMILY SUPPORTIVE?

Before entering bivocational ministry you must answer the question, Is your family supportive? Your secular job already demands a certain amount of your time. Other activities in which you are involved take additional time. Becoming a bivocational minister will take even more time away from your family. If your family is not supportive and if they do not sense the same call you do, there will be problems.

No one has been a greater supporter of my ministry than my wife. The eleven years I attended school meant I was away from home many evenings. When I was home, there were lessons to study, papers to write, sermons to prepare, and visits that needed to be made. I do not ever remember hearing one word of complaint. In fact, she constantly encouraged me to continue on in pursuit of my educational goals.

My wife is probably my greatest prayer warrior. She challenges me when she believes I am letting down in a particular area of ministry. Occasionally, she will mention that I need to increase the amount of time I spend doing visitation. She may even mention someone she believes needs a visit. I question her after each sermon because I know she will be honest with me. Every pastor needs a loving critic, and I have one of the best. When I have become so discouraged that I have been almost willing to give up, she has been the one to encourage me not to quit. She reminds me of how much good is being accomplished and how God is blessing the work that is being done. Hebron Baptist Church does not know how much they owe my wife because of the support she has given me over the years. I doubt that any church truly understands the valuable role the pastor's wife plays in the church.

If you have children, they also need to be supportive of your ministry. There will be times when ministry demands will cause you to miss some activity your children want you to attend. When they are younger, they may have problems understanding why you could not be there. However, if you make a great effort to be involved in their lives and in the activities that mean much to them, they will find it easier to understand when you have to be absent on occasion.

What should a person do if he feels called to bivocational ministry but his family is not supportive? I strongly suggest he not enter the ministry until there is agreement in the family. I believe the Bible teaches that the father is the spiritual leader of the home, but that does not mean he is not to receive guidance from the other members of the family. You are not the only one who can hear from God. It may be that other family members have correctly understood God's leading while you have misunderstood him. The Bible tells us that "by the mouth of two or three witnesses every word may be established" (Matt. 18:16).

If God has called you into bivocational ministry, he will confirm that calling through the support of your family. This should be a matter of family prayer until every member of the family is in genuine agreement with one another.

DO YOU HAVE THE GIFTS TO MINISTER IN A CHURCH?

Every Christian has been given spiritual gifts that are to be used in service to God. However, not all of those gifts will equip one to serve as a leader in a church. A pastor, for instance, needs certain gifts to fulfill the ministry he has been given.

I once introduced an individual who was considering bivocational ministry to a denominational leader. The leader told the individual that if he could preach, they could teach him how to baptize and marry and bury people. The implication was clear. There are some tasks a pastor does that can be learned while others can be successfully performed only with the proper gifts that come from God.

What gifts are necessary for a successful ministry? George Barna believes that "one of the indispensable characteristics of a ministry that transforms lives is leadership."[9] His research indicates that few pastors claim to have the gift of leadership, and of those who do, none feel that seminary prepared them for leadership in the church.[10] Leith Anderson agrees when he writes that "current demands on pastors focus on leadership, communication, administration, and interpersonal relationships. These skills often were not learned at seminary."[11]

If leadership skills are not learned in seminary, where can a pastor develop the leadership gifts God has given him? The bivocational pastor may learn these skills in his second job. Much time and money is being spent today by companies of every size to develop leadership skills in their employees. My former employer offered numerous classes as our company began to move to a new team-based work system. Training in conflict management, team building, responding to the needs of the customers, and how to conduct successful meetings were just some of the leadership classes they offered to their shop employees. All of them contained principles that were transferable to ministry situations.

Seminars are also available that can help one develop better leadership skills. Some of these are ministry related while others are directed toward the secular world. I have profited by attending both.

If you feel you have been called by God to serve him in a ministry position and your family supports you, if there is a need for a bivocational minister in your area, and if you have spiritual gifts that can be used in church ministry, then you need to seriously consider accepting God's call to bivocational ministry. Your pastor, church leaders, and family can help you sort through these questions to determine if God is calling you to this type of ministry. However, you alone must make the final decision based on what you believe God is saying to you.

WHAT ARE SOME ADVANTAGES YOU WOULD BRING TO A BIVOCATIONAL MINISTRY?

You're One of Them

A small church can often relate better to a bivocational pastor because he seems more real to them. Because their pastor works at a job just like the rest of the congregation, members view him as one of them.[12] Such a view is important in a small church because it reduces the amount of time it takes for trust to be established between the congregation and the minister. As we have seen in an earlier chapter, the sooner trust occurs, the sooner the church can begin to move forward.

Personal Experiences

You have experiences that no one else has, which is a valuable asset in sermon preparation. Illustrations are important to a sermon, and a number of resources contain illustrations that can help make a sermon clearer. But I believe these books are so popular because many pastors have few life experiences that can be used as illustrations.

I have served in the military, farmed, sold seed corn, worked thirty years in a factory, and now I run my own company. Most of the illustrations I use come from real-life situations that I have observed in my experiences. Those experiences often add credibility to my sermons. When I talk about employer-employee relationships, the congregation knows I have been on both sides of that situation. I can personally relate to many of Jesus' parables in which he referred to agricultural practices and so can the members of our rural church.

My congregation knows I came to Christ later in life than some and that alcohol was a part of my life before I was saved. Now when I minister to someone who is fighting alcohol's influence, that person knows I once experienced some of the things he or she is now going through. I can explain how Jesus Christ set me free from the desire for alcohol and that he can set others free as well.

Scripture tells us that when Jesus finished the Sermon on the Mount the crowds were amazed because he spoke with more authority than did the Scribes (Matt. 7:28–29). When the Scribes taught, they constantly referred to the teachings and interpretation of Scripture from earlier rabbinical teaching. Their authority rested on the authority of those they quoted. Jesus taught the people simply and directly and used everyday illustrations they could easily understand. He illustrated profound truths using his and his listeners' own experiences.

Nobody else has had the experiences you have had, and those unique experiences can help you greatly as you minister to other people. They can serve as illustrations that add meaning to your sermons. They allow you to minister with more empathy to those who may be going through similar experiences. Finally, your experiences add authority to your ministry.

Knowledge of Community

Another advantage you bring to the ministry is your knowledge of the community. As I told the pulpit committee at Hebron, I may not have the education and experience that others have, but I do know where the hospital is, and I know where most of the members live. That familiarity with the community has advantages beyond knowing where places are located.

You may know some of the movers and shakers in your community. In fact, you may be working with some of them in your other job. These people can be an asset to your ministry because they can help make things happen in your church. They can also be excellent sources for referral when you are not able to help a member of your church with a problem.

Before I took early retirement, I served on my employer's community relations committee. Our company was committed to community service, and we provided financial support to worthwhile endeavors in the community. Each month we would meet to discuss various funding requests, and we often invited an organization to give us an overview of what services it provided. During my time on this committee, I developed a better understanding of the work that many of these organizations were doing. This knowledge has enabled me to give better referrals to people who have specific needs our church could not meet.

Of course, here I am assuming that you are a bivocational minister in the community in which you live. Some bivocational ministers do move elsewhere to serve a church, but I sense that a large number of bivocational ministers are serving in areas in which they are already working and living. If that is the case, your knowledge of your community is a valuable asset as you begin your ministry.

Relationships with Unchurched People

Another advantage you bring is the influence you have over unchurched people. I have had people who have been Christians for a long time tell me they have no friends who are not Christians. Some pastors are no different. As one who works in the world, you will be working daily with a number of people who are not associated with a church.

One of the first things a missionary does when he begins serving in a location is to become friends with the people. He learns their language, their habits and customs, their likes and dislikes, their beliefs and values, and their needs. Only after learning these things can he effectively minister to them.

As a bivocational minister, you will be working and living every day in the culture that you are wanting to influence for Christ. You already know the language and customs. You understand the values and beliefs. Working alongside non-Christians, you will certainly understand their needs because their needs will often be similar to your needs. You can have a powerful testimony to them as you relate how God has met those needs in your life through Jesus Christ.

Bivocational ministry is not for everyone. Perhaps most of those God calls into ministry are called to be fully supported by a church. But as we have seen, many churches cannot afford to call this type of pastor. I personally believe that God is going to raise up even more bivocational pastors to minister to these churches in the future. Perhaps he is calling you to be one of these pastors.

If God has called you to bivocational ministry, give him thanks for the opportunity to serve him in a very rewarding way. Pray about which church he may be leading you to serve. Love the people in that church and feel that love returned to you in many ways. Seek God's vision for that church. Share that vision with the church and help the members achieve it. When God begins to do great things in that church, thank him again for calling you to such a wonderful ministry.

NINE

BIVOCATIONAL MINISTRY MAY BE FOR YOUR CHURCH

In this final chapter, I want to address church leaders in particular. It is my hope that this book will be read not only by bivocational ministers and those considering such a ministry but also by denominational and church leaders as they seek new pastors for their small churches. I want to challenge you to consider calling a bivocational pastor to lead your church.

There are two types of churches I will primarily be addressing. The first is the very small church (Sunday morning attendance of less than fifty people) who knows it cannot afford a fully supported pastor. These churches are often served by student pastors or retired pastors, who come and go quite often. The second type of church averages 51 to 100 people on Sunday morning and has traditionally had a fully supported pastor and believes it must continue to be served by one. Their pastors also frequently leave after a relatively short period of ministry.

The median base yearly salary for a pastor of the first type of church is $16,560.[1] Few people would expect a pastor to be able to live on that salary for very long. Unfortunately, the salary level does not increase much for a pastor who leads a church with 51 to 100 people in attendance. The median base salary for this pastor is only $20,904.[2] What does change is that quite often a church this size does expect its pastor to be able to live on this salary without any other source of income.

Let's examine the realities of this situation. Quite often the pastor of a church this size will be a young person who has recently graduated from seminary. It is possible that he has finished school with an educational debt of $10,000 to $30,000, which he must now begin repaying. He is probably married. The couple may already have children or is thinking about starting a family. How long will he and his family be able to live on a salary of less than $21,000? Within a few years, financial need will dictate that this pastor find a larger church that is able to more adequately support him and his family.

A pastor search committee recently contacted me asking if I would be interested in meeting with them. This church averages seventy-five people at the morning worship service. The chairwoman of the committee told me the church had a great amount of potential but had seen a declining attendance over the past few years. They also were having trouble keeping a pastor for more than three or four years. One reason they contacted me was because of the length of time I had been at Hebron. The committee believed the church would not reach its potential unless it kept a pastor for an extended period of time.

They were offering a salary package of $25,000 and a small parsonage. If the church grew, they would be glad to increase that salary, but they did not want their pastor to supplement his income by working another job.

I believe that a church of this size would be better served by calling a bivocational pastor who would be able to stay with the church for a long period of time to provide the leadership the church needs. It is time for churches to put their pride behind them and realize that their expectations of having a fully supported pastor are no longer feasible. Such expectations not only do a disservice to a pastor and his family, they also prevent the church from having a more effective ministry. A bivocational pastor offers several advantages to a small church that the members need to consider.

THE ADVANTAGES OF HAVING
A BIVOCATIONAL PASTOR

More Resources Are Available for Ministry

A basic economic principle is that all resources are limited. Any time a resource is used for one purpose it cannot be used for another. Churches have limited amounts of money that can be used for ministry. Money that is spent for ministerial support is not available for other programs. Any time a congregation spends more than 40 percent of its budget on ministerial compensation, other programs, ministries, and building maintenance are often underfinanced.[3]

Too often, churches have adopted a backdoor approach to this problem. They have decided what they want to spend on programs and ministry, and the pastor gets what is left. I know one pastor who was told that the church wanted to increase his salary but couldn't because the members wanted to add additional programs to the church's ministry. The members probably did not realize it, but they were telling their pastor they would be funding these programs with the salary increases he would not be receiving! The Bible is clear that the church is to provide proper compensation for its leaders. Pastors should not have to finance the ministry of the church with what should be part of their salaries.

A bivocational pastor and his family could enjoy a higher standard of living by receiving part of its income from a job outside the church, and the church would have more funds with which to support its ministry. Read chapter 5 again and look at all the ministries our church has been able to do. We've had the ability to do these things because an excessive amount of our budget does not go toward pastoral compensation.

Longer Pastorates

Much time has been spent throughout this book discussing the advantages of longer pastorates, so there is no need to go into detail here. Quite simply, a church usually does better when it has a pastor for a longer period of time because effective pastoral ministry usually does not occur during the first few years of ministry. A church and a pastor need time to develop trust in one another. It also takes time for a church and a pastor to reach a common vision for the church. Until this trust and vision are established, the church will make little progress.

Bivocational pastors often stay at their churches for long periods of time. Economic factors are only one reason why this is true. A bivocational pastor often has deep ties to the community in which he lives, works, and serves. His extended family may also live in the community. Regardless of the reason, a church will usually benefit from the more effective ministry often associated with long pastorates.

More Is Expected of the Laypeople

At first, this may seem to be a strange benefit, but that is only because we have confused the proper roles of the pastor and the laity. Church is not a spectator sport. Too often, in small churches the laypeople consider the pastor to be the one responsible for all the ministry in the church. Visitation is done by the pastor. Evangelism is the pastor's responsibility. He may also teach Sunday school and lead the youth group.

While conducting a revival a few years ago, I met an individual who graduated from Bible school with me. Following graduation, he had taken the pastorate of a church in another state. He had already left that church and moved back. Everything done in that church was his responsibility. After the service one Sunday morning a lady complained to him that a light was burned out in the women's bathroom. He asked why she was telling him, and she replied, "So you can fix it. That's what we pay you for!"

Such a mind-set is possible in a small church because some people believe that a fully supported pastor in a church with 50 to 100 members is underemployed.[4] If a pastor does many of the things that the laypeople should be doing for themselves, however, he is not fulfilling his ministerial responsibilities and is doing spiritual harm to his congregation.

In Ephesians 4 God makes it clear that he has called some into the ministry in order to equip his people for the work of ministry. The role of the pastor is to teach, to lead, and to encourage the members of the congregation to use the gifts God has given them so they can perform the ministries he has given them. A pastor shortchanges a congregation if he does all the work himself. Likewise, church members harm themselves when they expect the pastor to do all the work of ministry.

A bivocational pastor simply does not have time to do all the work that needs to be done in a church. Most people in a bivocational church understand that and are more willing to help. Several years ago I was preparing the bulletins when a woman asked if she could take over that responsibility. I haven't had to type the bulletins since. Our deacons are good about visiting our sick and shut-ins. A few weeks ago I noticed a problem on the exterior of our building and mentioned it to one of our trustees. He had already noticed the problem, spoken to the other trustees, and arranged to have the problem fixed.

Many bivocational pastors and churches find it helpful to develop a "covenant for ministry."[5] The pastor and the leaders of the congregation determine what tasks need to be done in the church and how many hours the pastor can provide. If more hours are needed than the pastor can give, the church leaders recruit others within the church to provide the extra hours. This covenant should be written and reviewed periodically.

A covenant for ministry can accomplish several things. It provides an excellent means by which a church can evaluate the effectiveness of its minister. Too often, such evaluations are subjective with everyone evaluating the minister based on what he or she believes should be his priorities. A covenant lists the agreed upon priorities to which the minister is to commit the bulk of his ministry time. It also informs the congregation of the time limitations that the bivocational pastor has for ministry purposes. Finally, it allows the bivocational pastor to focus on the ministry tasks the church has stated are his responsibility. Such focus eliminates some of the stress that ministers often feel when confronted with several ministry tasks that are in need of attention.

Small churches seldom give careful consideration to what they really need in a pastor. When their pastor leaves, they want to replace him immediately. They may contact the nearest seminary or their denominational support person and ask for names of available ministers. Little thought is given to what skills the church needs in a new pastor. They simply want a preacher to fill their pulpit as quickly as possible. What such a church often really needs is "a professional leader who will become an enabler, helping the people of the church to assume more responsibility and leadership."[6]

Leighton Ford wrote, "It has been said the final test of a leader is that he leaves behind others who have the conviction and the will to carry on."[7] When a new pastor comes to lead Hebron Baptist Church, he will find the members are capable and willing to do the work of ministry. Because of that willingness, we have been able to do much more than if I had tried to do everything myself.

The Possibility of Hiring More Staff

Sometimes a church simply does not have laypeople with the gifts and/or the time for certain ministries. Even a pastor is not gifted to do every type of ministry in a church, and if he is in a somewhat larger church, he will not have the time to lead every ministry. Some churches are finding that they can add additional staff by using bivocational ministers to lead specific ministries within their church.[8]

We did this at Hebron several years ago. The church was concerned about a lack of youth in the church. The main reason we had no youth in our church was that we had nothing for the youth. Our youth program had been led by laypeople for several years, but the leaders grew tired of the work, and no one wanted to take their places. Everyone in the church felt they lacked either the necessary gifts or the time to lead a youth group. I also did not have the time for another responsibility, nor did I feel I had the right gifts. We knew that until we offered the area youth a reason to attend our church, we would never draw in the many young people of the community.

At a business meeting one evening, I suggested that we consider hiring a part-time youth minister. This person could be a student at the seminary or bivocational. Everyone agreed we should look into that possibility. We formed a committee to prepare a job description and establish a salary package to present to the church. This committee later became the search committee, and within a few months, we called a young man to lead our youth program.

Other churches in our area were stunned. Hebron Baptist Church, with an average attendance of approximately forty people, had two ministers on staff! People from churches larger than ours called, wanting to know how we could afford two ministers. They also wanted a youth minister but did not believe they could afford one. I explained that our church had two bivocational ministers whose combined wages and benefits were much less than their one fully supported pastor. Some of the churches who contacted me were marginal in their need for a fully supported pastor. Perhaps they would have been better served with two bivocational ministers who could meet the specific needs of their churches.

A bivocational minister may even be a good choice for a larger church with a fully supported pastor. Such a church may have a need for leadership for their youth, their music program, or their educational program. Sometimes a church will add one staff person who is responsible for all these tasks, but this person may not have the spiritual gifts needed for each of these ministries. Often, one or more areas will suffer while the staff minister concentrates on the ministry for which he is gifted. The church could solve this problem by calling a bivocational minister for each of the positions that need to be filled.

A Pastor Who Can Relate

Church members sometimes complain that their pastor lives in an ivory tower world and does not understand real life and the problems that real people face every day. In some cases they are right. Pastors often have life experiences that differ from those of many in their congregation. Although pastors experience various pressures in their profession, pastoral ministry is not the same as working in a factory or in sales or in any other profession. A pastor usually works within a church setting with other people who speak the language of the church and hold to the same beliefs he does. Even when working with people outside the church, those people will often watch what they say or do in deference to his position. A pastor may have little idea of how difficult it can be to be a positive Christian witness while working on an assembly line with a group of people who do not hold to, or even respect, Christian values.

A member of my church worked all his life in construction. A few years ago he became a Christian. Several times he has remarked how hard it is to consistently live his life in accordance with his new values. He struggles to watch his language, especially when he gets hurt on the job. When problems arise on the job, he works hard to maintain a positive attitude and not respond in an inappropriate way. He does these things because he knows that his fellow workers are watching him to see if his life matches his new faith.

Because of my life's experiences and the years I worked in a factory while a bivocational minister, I can identify with the struggles he faces. I can also identify with the times he has lost those battles because I lost a few of them as well. Being bivocational, I bring a different perspective to my preaching and my counseling. Many churches would benefit from that perspective.

A bivocational pastor can also understand why church members cannot be at the church for some function or activity every night of the week. Too many churches have something scheduled seven nights a week. In small churches, members are frequently asked to fill three or four positions within the church, and then those doing the asking complain when their requests are turned down. A lack of commitment to God and to the church is the usual charge.

Sometimes the problem is that the pastor, who often works at the church six or seven days a week, does not understand that the members of the church have a life outside the church. They are working forty or more hours a week. Family responsibilities take additional time. They have only so much time available to give to the ministry of the church. A bivocational pastor understands because he also balances the demands of a full-time job and the responsibilities of family life.

A few years ago I noticed that our people appeared to be exhausted. It was the first night of Vacation Bible School, and I could see that everyone was already tired. We had just been recognized for the second time as the church of the year by our state denominational office. The members had worked very hard for an extended period of time to accomplish a number of good things in our church. Now, they were tired.

I remarked to my wife on the way home that evening that everyone needed some time to rest. I made the decision that when Vacation Bible School was finished, we were going to take a break. I was not going to ask anyone in the church to do anything else for the rest of the year. We would start no new programs. We literally went into a holding pattern for the last half of the year as everyone was given time to rest. The church did not suffer, everyone had time to be refreshed, and the following year we resumed our active ministry.

THE DISADVANTAGES OF HAVING A BIVOCATIONAL PASTOR

So far, we have discussed only the advantages a church may experience with a bivocational pastor. While they are many, there are also some disadvantages. We need to address them now.

Lack of Immediate Availability

Perhaps the first one that comes to mind is a lack of immediate availability. This can be important in case of a death, an accident, or a serious illness. A member may want the pastor present immediately but be unable to contact him. A member may be facing emergency surgery, but the pastor doesn't find out about it until arriving home after work. These situations are real possibilities, but, fortunately, they do not happen very often in a small church. In eighteen years, I have encountered only a couple situations in which my presence was needed by a member of the church while I was at work. In those cases, my wife relayed the information to me, and I was able to leave work to minister to the situation. Because the members understand my bivocational status, they usually will ask me to contact them when I get home from work. This has allowed me to provide responsible ministry to almost every need and yet be quickly available in those rare instances when my immediate presence is needed.

Weakened Denominational Ties

A bivocational pastor will not have much time to be involved in denominational activities. Ministerial meetings will often be held during the day while he is at work. Other denominational meetings will often be held at a central location that may be a distance from the pastor's home. While trying to juggle all his other responsibilities, a bivocational pastor will often see denominational work as something for which he does not have time. His attitude may well be, "Let the big churches deal with that stuff. I've got all I can do to take care of our little church." Such an attitude, while understandable, can weaken a church's ties to its denomination.

To be honest, this is not just a problem for bivocational churches. It has long been noted in our area that churches who depend on student pastors also have this problem. The student pastors often adopt the same attitude as many bivocational pastors. As a result, small churches are often not even aware of what the denomination is doing. Denominational mailings are often sent to the church office. If the pastor is not interested, that information seldom finds its way to the members of the church.

There are some steps a bivocational church can take to resolve this problem. One is to ask that denominational mailings be sent to a lay leader's address rather than to the church. This could be especially important if the church has had a series of short-term pastorates, if the church has a student pastor, or if the church has a pastor with a different denominational background than that of the church.

Another remedy is to subscribe to several copies of the denomination's newsletters and magazines so that various lay leaders in the church receive a copy. These materials will often inform the church about what the denomination is doing and what programs it is offering. Subscriptions for these are usually inexpensive, and their value will far outweigh the cost. Lay leaders in the church also need to know the denomination's representative for their church. This person's phone number and address should be available, and regular contact should be made with this individual. If the pastor does not inform the church about denominational activities, it may be helpful to invite the denominational representative to the church at least once a year to provide an update on those activities. In this way, the church can maintain its denominational identity and also likely encourage denominational support.

It is not too much for a church to ask its pastor to find some level of involvement in the work of the denomination. Quite frankly, I have a problem with some pastors who are willing to accept the financial support of the church and yet do not support the denomination of that church. I personally believe that shows a lack of integrity on the part of the pastor. A bivocational minister has an obligation as a pastor of a denominational church to maintain some involvement in denominational activities.

I certainly understand that a bivocational pastor does not have a lot of time for denominational work, but he must make some time available. I have not attended every annual state convention, but I have attended several. I just returned from attending our denomination's biennial meeting. When American Baptists had a capital fund-raising effort a few years ago, I served as a mission cluster director and was responsible for educating and assisting seven churches in their efforts to raise money for mission work. Our church benefits from my occasional involvement in the work of our denomination because it strengthens our ties with the denomination. A bivocational church does not have to see its denominational ties weakened because it has bivocational leadership. Such a church simply needs to insist that its pastor inform them of denominational activity, and the church needs to take personal responsibility to find ways to stay informed as well.

The Church Has Only a Preacher and Not a Pastor

Sometimes a bivocational church has a minister who is only a preacher and not a pastor. Such an individual sees preparing and delivering sermons as his only responsibility. He does no visitation or counseling. He frequently does not attend meetings. He does not lead the church in planning, goal setting, or seeking God's vision for the future.

This person has either a wrong concept of bivocational ministry, or he has not been called into pastoral ministry at all. Being bivocational does not mean second-rate efforts are acceptable. Bivocational ministry involves providing real ministry to a church, and preaching is only one aspect of that ministry. Churches need pastors, not just preachers, to minister to them and to lead them.

The disadvantages of having a bivocational pastor can be real, but many of them can be overcome. For a small church, the advantages of having a bivocational pastor will often far outweigh the disadvantages. The longer pastorate usually associated with bivocational ministry may be the best advantage of all to a church that has experienced a series of short-term pastors. A longer ministry may be the catalyst that allows your church to move forward into the ministry God has planned for your church.

NOTES

PREFACE

1. Darrell Robinson, *Missions USA* (November–December 1993): 54.

2. Michael Green, *Evangelism through the Local Church* (Nashville: Oliver Nelson, 1990), xii.

CHAPTER 1

1. George Barna, *Today's Pastors* (Ventura, Calif.: Regal Books, 1993), 37.

2. Donald Grey Barnhouse, *Romans,* vol. 1 (Grand Rapids: Eerdmans, 1952), preface.

3. W. A. Criswell, *Criswell's Guidebook for Pastors* (Nashville: Broadman Press, 1980), 75.

4. Ronald Klassen and John Koessler, *No Little Places: The Untapped Potential of the Small-Town Church* (Grand Rapids: Baker, 1996), 35.

5. David L. Goetz, "The Truth about Debt and Salaries," *Leadership* (spring 1997): 87.

6. Barna, *Today's Pastors,* 37.

7. Dale Holloway, "From Where I Stand," *The Bivocational Beacon* (spring 1996).

8. Darius Salter, *What Really Matters in Ministry* (Grand Rapids: Baker, 1990), 33.

9. Doran McCarty, *Leading the Small Church* (Nashville: Broadman Press, 1991), 98.

10. Klassen and Koessler, *No Little Places,* 35.

11. Leith Anderson, *A Church for the Twenty-First Century* (Minneapolis: Bethany, 1992), 213.

12. John MacArthur Jr., *Our Sufficiency in Christ* (Dallas: Word, 1991), 153–56.

13. Rick Warren, *The Purpose Driven Church* (Grand Rapids: Zondervan, 1995), 295.

14. Luther M. Door, *The Bivocational Pastor* (Nashville: Broadman Press, 1988), 66.

CHAPTER 2

1. George Barna, *Today's Pastors* (Ventura, Calif.: Regal Books, 1993), 39.

2. "One Call—Two Ministries," *The Bivocational Beacon* (spring 1996).

3. "Bivocational Pastors Play Significant Role in SBC," *Research Review* (summer 1993): 1.

4. John Caldwell, "We're in Good Company," *The Bivocational Beacon* (fall 1996).

5. Lyle E. Schaller, *It's a Different World!: The Challenge for Today's Pastor* (Nashville: Abingdon Press, 1987), 80.

6. Arnell P. C. Arn, *The Alive in Mission New Church Planting Decade Report* (Valley Forge, Pa.: American Baptist Churches USA, n.d.), 4.

7. Ibid., 12.

8. "Bivocational Pastors," 4.

9. Barna, *Today's Pastors,* 32.

10. Schaller, *It's a Different World,* 204.

11. Lyle E. Schaller, "The Shrinking Middle," *The Parish Paper* (1997), 1.

12. George Barna, *Turnaround Churches* (Ventura, Calif.: Regal Books, 1993), 43.

Notes

13. H. B. London Jr. and Neil B. Wiseman, *Your Pastor Is an Endangered Species* (Wheaton: Victor Books, 1996), 12.

14. Robert Hicks, *Uneasy Manhood* (Nashville: Oliver Nelson, 1991), 66.

15. Leith Anderson, *A Church for the Twenty-First Century* (Minneapolis: Bethany, 1992), 46.

16. Lyle Schaller, *The Small Church Is Different!* (Nashville: Abingdon Press, 1982), 42.

17. Anderson, *Church for the Twenty-First Century*, 63–64.

18. "Happenings around the Country," *The Bivocational Beacon* (fall 1996).

CHAPTER 3

1. George Barna, *Today's Pastors* (Ventura, Calif.: Regal Books, 1993), 59.

2. R. Kent Hughes, *Disciplines of a Godly Man* (Wheaton: Crossway Books, 1991), 151.

3. Carl F. H. Henry, *Aspects of Christian Social Ethics* (Grand Rapids: Eerdmans, 1964), 40.

4. Hughes, *Disciplines*, 152–54.

5. Luther M. Dorr, *The Bivocational Pastor* (Nashville: Broadman Press, 1988), 74.

6. Ibid.

7. Dale Holloway, "From Where I Stand," *The Bivocational Beacon* (spring 1996).

8. David L. Goetz, "Forced Out," *Leadership* (winter 1996): 42.

9. Dorr, *Bivocational Pastor*, 73.

10. Barna, *Today's Pastors*, 61ff.

11. Ron Klassen and John Koessler, *No Little Places: The Untapped Potential of the Small-Town Church* (Grand Rapids: Baker, 1996), 25.

12. H. B. London Jr. and Neil B. Wiseman, *The Heart of a Great Pastor* (Ventura, Calif.: Regal Books, 1994), 20.

13. J. H. Jowett, *The Preacher, His Life and Work* (New York: George H. Doran Company, 1912), 12.

14. Doran C. McCarty, "The Glory of the Call," in *Meeting the Challenge of Bivocational Ministry*, ed. Doran C. McCarty (Nashville: Seminary Extension, 1996), 88.

CHAPTER **4**

1. Lyle E. Schaller, *It's a Different World!: The Challenge for Today's Pastor* (Nashville: Abingdon Press, 1987), 180–96.

2. Don Davidson, *How to Build an Exciting Singles Ministry . . . And Keep It Going* (Nashville: Thomas Nelson, 1993).

3. George Barna, *The Frog in the Kettle* (Ventura, Calif.: Regal Books, 1990), 142–43.

4. Ibid., 133–35.

5. Schaller, *It's a Different World,* 24–33.

6. Lyle E. Schaller, *The New Reformation: Tomorrow Arrived Yesterday* (Nashville: Abingdon Press, 1995), 124.

7. Leith Anderson, *A Church for the Twenty-First Century* (Minneapolis: Bethany, 1992), 46.

8. George Barna, *Today's Pastors* (Ventura, Calif.: Regal Books, 1993), 126.

9. John Throop, "Get Your Degree Online," *Your Church* (September/October 1998): 114.

10. James Nelson, "The Bivocational Issue," in *Meeting the Challenge of Bivocational Ministry,* ed. Doran C. McCarty (Nashville: Seminary Extension, 1996), 105.

11. George Clark, "Special Problems of Bivocational Ministers," in *Meeting the Challenge of Bivocational Ministry,* 244.

12. W. A. Criswell, *Criswell's Guidebook for Pastors* (Nashville: Broadman Press, 1980), 64.

13. Ibid., 68.

14. Alexandr Solzhenitsyn, *Christianity Today,* 13 September 1993, 96.

15. H. B. London and Neil B. Wiseman, *The Heart of a Great Pastor* (Ventura, Calif.: Regal Books, 1994), 180.

16. Richard J. Foster, *Celebration of Discipline,* rev. ed. (San Francisco: Harper & Row, 1988), 62.

17. Ibid., 71ff.

CHAPTER **5**

1. Leon Wilson, personal interview, 14 August 1997.

2. Paul O. Madsen, *The Small Church: Valid, Vital, Victorious* (Valley Forge, Pa.: Judson Press, 1975), 48.

3. Ibid., 45.

4. Ron Klassen and John Koessler, *No Little Places: The Untapped Potential of the Small-Town Church* (Grand Rapids: Baker, 1996), 35.

5. George C. Hunter III, *Church for the Unchurched* (Nashville: Abingdon Press, 1996), 134.

6. Rick Warren, *The Purpose Driven Church* (Grand Rapids: Zondervan, 1995), 384–85.

7. Hunter, *Church for the Unchurched,* 140.

CHAPTER 6

1. Billy Graham, *Just As I Am* (New York: HarperCollins, 1997), 723.

2. Bill and Lynne Hybels, *Fit to Be Tied* (Grand Rapids: Zondervan, 1991), 151ff; and *Rediscovering Church: The Story and Vision of Willow Creek Community Church* (Grand Rapids: Zondervan, 1995), 44.

3. W. A. Criswell, *Criswell's Guidebook for Pastors* (Nashville: Broadman Press, 1980), 348.

4. H. B. London Jr. and Neil B. Wiseman, *The Heart of a Great Pastor* (Ventura, Calif.: Regal Books, 1994), 180.

5. Jim Conway, *Men in Midlife Crisis* (Elgin, Ill.: David C. Cook, 1978).

6. Richard A. Swenson, *Margin* (Colorado Springs: Navpress, 1992), 92.

7. Ibid., 100.

8. Ibid., 30.

9. J. Grant Howard, *Balancing Life's Demands* (Sisters, Ore.: Multnomah, 1994), 98.

CHAPTER 7

1. Charles R. Swindoll, *Laugh Again* (Dallas: Word, 1992), 14.

2. John MacArthur Jr., *Rediscovering Expository Preaching* (Dallas: Word, 1992), xv.

3. W. A. Criswell, *Criswell's Guidebook for Pastors* (Nashville: Broadman Press, 1980), 60.

4. The Ministers and Missionaries Benefit Board of American Baptist Churches, *1997 Questions and Answers for Church Treasurers* (New York: M&M, 1996), 12.

5. Charles R. Swindoll, *Rise and Shine* (Portland, Ore.: Multnomah, 1989), 47.

CHAPTER 8

1. "Happenings around the Country," *The Bivocational Beacon* (fall 1996).

2. Howard F. Sugden and Warren W. Wiersbe, *Confident Pastoral Leadership,* 2d ed. (Grand Rapids: Baker, 1993), 13.

3. Ibid., 14.

4. W. A. Criswell, *Standing on the Promises* (Dallas: Word, 1990), 37–39.

5. Charles R. Swindoll, *Rise and Shine* (Portland, Ore.: Multnomah, 1989), 217–18.

6. Franklin M. Segler, *A Theology of Church and Ministry* (Nashville: Broadman Press, 1960), 50.

7. George Barna, *Today's Pastors* (Ventura, Calif.: Regal Books, 1993), 40.

8. George Barna, *Turnaround Churches* (Ventura, Calif.: Regal Books, 1993), 34.

9. Barna, *Today's Pastors,* 117.

10. Ibid., 126.

11. Leith Anderson, *A Church for the Twenty-First Century* (Minneapolis: Bethany, 1992), 75.

12. Luther M. Door, *The Bivocational Pastor* (Nashville: Broadman Press, 1988), 68.

CHAPTER 9

1. David L. Goetz, "The Truth about Debt and Salaries," *Leadership* (spring 1997): 87.

2. Ibid.

3. Lyle E. Schaller, *The Small Church Is Different* (Nashville: Abingdon Press, 1982), 85.

4. John Y. Elliott, *Our Pastor Has an Outside Job* (Valley Forge, Pa.: Judson Press, 1980), 15.

5. Gary Farley and Dale Holloway, "Shared Ministry and the Bivocational Minister," in *Meeting the Challenge of Bivocational Ministry,* ed. Doran C. McCarty (Nashville: Seminary Extension, 1996), 181.

6. Paul O. Madsen, *The Small Church: Valid, Vital, Victorious* (Valley Forge, Pa.: Judson Press, 1975), 37.

7. Leighton Ford, "Helping Leaders Grow," in *Leaders on Leadership,* ed. George Barna (Ventura, Calif.: Regal Books, 1997), 127.

8. Elliott, *Our Pastor,* 14.

Dennis W. Bickers is a bivocational pastor who worked for Cummins Engine Company and is owner of Madison Heating and Air Conditioning in Madison, Indiana. He serves as pastor of Hebron Baptist Church, which has twice received the church of the year award from the American Baptist Churches of Indiana. He is a graduate of Boyce Bible School of Southern Baptist Theological Seminary in Louisville and Indiana University Southeast in New Albany, Indiana.